Our **Gay** Son

A Christian Father's Search for Truth

David Robert-John

authorHOUSE®

AuthorHouse™
1663 Liberty Drive
Bloomington, IN 47403
www.authorhouse.com
Phone: 1-800-839-8640

All Scripture quotations in this publication are from THE HOLY BIBLE, NEW INTERNATIONAL VERSION®, NIV® Copyright © 1973, 1978, 1984, 2011 by Biblica, Inc.™ Used by permission. All rights reserved worldwide.

First published by AuthorHouse   01/04/2012

ISBN: 978-1-4678-8599-7 (sc)
ISBN: 978-1-4678-8598-0 (ebk)

Printed in the United States of America

The author wishes to express his gratitude to the following organisations for kind permission to quote extracts from their publications:

The Royal College of Psychiatrists (Submission to the Church of England's Listening Exercise on Human Sexuality).
www.rcpsych.ac.uk/Submission%20to%20the%20Church%20of%20England.pdf

Inter–Varsity Press (Walking with Gay Friends—Alex Tylee)

The Lutterworth Press (*Homosexuality: A New Christian Ethic - Dr. Elizabeth R. Moberly*)

Dedication

To my three children, in particular my gay son. I shall always be indebted to you for what you have taught me.

Also

to my wife, whose love gives me the will to carry on.

Contents

Acknowledgements

Grateful thanks are due to four people in particular:

Helen Collins, for her constant encouragement and her suggestion that the original book be split into two, this book and the sequel *Homosexuality: The Bible on Trial*.

Roderick Thomson, a colleague at my last school for his interest, advice and support.

David Stokes, another colleague at the same school, who checked the manuscript for mistakes (he found many). Unfortunately, when amending my script, I had new inspiration, added further material and changed other parts. Any errors that crept in at this late stage are entirely my responsibility.

David Callaghan for his invaluable help with the intricacies of Microsoft Word.

Preface

This book was written originally as a cathartic exercise. Perhaps I needed some way in which I could communicate things to my son that are not easy to say face to face. I also needed to become clear in my own mind about the journey that I had made and the point at which I had arrived.

Once I had started to write, however, the project became an obsession and I wrote far more than I had originally intended. Friends who read some of the early parts encouraged me to carry on and later to publish the complete book. This is the result, though it describes only the first part of the journey that I made. The rest of the story is told in a follow-up book.

When I had finished, both my wife and son were persuaded to write short contributions and share their own experiences of a journey that, in a sense, we made together, even if at times we seemed to be travelling along different paths. I learned a great deal from what they wrote: my son's perception of the person that I was differed greatly from the person that I thought I was. I hope that their contributions have helped to provide a more complete and balanced picture.

In its final form, it is intended first and foremost for any parent struggling to come to terms with having a gay child and particularly those of religious persuasion. It should also be of special interest to all those concerned about the "debate" on homosexuality within the Anglican Church as well as to anyone whose religious beliefs condemn homosexuality.

David Robert-John (December 2011)

Chapter 1   A DREAM DESTROYED

Boxing Day (December 26), 2005, is a day that will be forever etched in my memory. It is the day that my wife and I received the news that was to turn our lives upside down. We had had no premonition of the dramatic event that was about to unfold. Our three grown-up children were at home for the short Christmas break and they had been out until late the previous evening, catching up with old school friends. For that reason we were not expecting them to surface until later that morning. These days, our Jack Russell dog was all that we normally had to worry about. She was an early riser and had trained her owners to fit in with her lifestyle.

We were very contented parents, proud and grateful that our children had safely negotiated the turbulent teenage years and had gone on to exceed all our expectations at university. They could now boast of having better qualifications than I had managed to acquire nearly forty years earlier, although I insisted that this was because standards were no longer what they used to be. Nevertheless it is a significant point in a child's life if they are able to achieve this happy position.

Meanwhile, we were trying to adjust to the fact that they all lived some distance away and were no longer dependent on us. Occasional and fleeting visits were now all that we were able to count on. My wife found this more difficult than I did. She is Peruvian and in the community in which she grew up, children left home only when they got married. Our children had been brought up in a different country, they belonged to a more modern generation and marriage seemed a long way from their thoughts. My wife, who already had grandchildren on her mind, had been obliged to put her dreams on hold for the time being.

We had spent the previous day at the house of my elder brother, an Anglican vicar, and his wife. They lived an hour's drive away, but they had the advantage of living in a modern parsonage with enough room to accommodate all of our extended family, and some friends besides, for Christmas dinner. The day had passed in an atmosphere of happiness and tranquillity, although trying to recreate the magic of Christmas without the presence of young children is a rather difficult challenge. Appearances, however, can be deceptive, as we were very shortly to discover. Within twenty-four hours our world was to fall apart and one of our most cherished dreams would lie in ruins. We were, without being aware of the fact, experiencing the last day of peace and contentment that we were to know for a very long time.

Like most mothers, my wife found it difficult to accept that her children had become adults and she fretted perpetually about their wellbeing. Of particular concern was the idea that they would not be eating properly now that they were no longer getting regular doses of her delicious, though always health-conscious meals. Her mind was focussed on the breakfast she was waiting to prepare for them, and also probably on the evening meal, because that would be her last chance to stave off malnutrition for a little while longer. The fact that they might still be digesting the previous day's ample supply of food did not seem to occur to her, nor the fact that they had been looking after themselves perfectly well ever since leaving home to go to university some years earlier.

They would spend most the day doing their customary Boxing Day sales-shopping in the city that was a short train journey from the railway station close to where we live. Our two boys would be leaving us in the evening and our daughter would be going early the next morning. We wanted to make the most of the two mealtimes we had left as a family.

Normally, on these rare occasions when all our children stayed overnight, we would have expected them to appear for breakfast one at a time. My wife did not mind this as it enabled her to give them individual attention. However, we were surprised by the sound of footsteps on the stairs which indicated that they were coming down together. As soon as they entered the dining room, it was clear that they had something serious to tell us. It was our 22 year old younger son, flanked by his brother and sister, who spoke: "*Mum and dad, I have something to tell you,*" he began. There was a pause before he finished the sentence by adding "*I'm GAY.*"

I cannot find any words that are adequate to describe the impact of that shattering revelation. There may be people who would find this attitude astonishing in the present day and wonder where I had been living for most of my life. The answer to that question is that a lot of my time had been spent among evangelical Christians.

It is very easy for people to theorise about how they might react on being told such news by one of their children. I have a friend who works as a lecturer in a university, where, she tells me, there are many gay academic staff and a very liberal, accepting atmosphere. She comes from a family with a strong Catholic background, although she prides herself on being open about the question of religion and on having modern, liberal views about sexuality. Yet when her eldest son, at sixteen years of age, told her that he was gay, she admitted that she cried for a week. Liberal views are easy to hold as long as the problem is not your own. Sadly, when the problem does become your own, you begin to realize, or perhaps you are obliged to acknowledge, just how much ignorance and prejudice still exists in the world.

Whatever anyone imagines their own views on homosexuality to be, they will become aware that there are others who will regard a homosexual child as somehow "faulty". They will also realise that a homosexual child belongs to a minority group and this brings its own hardships. My wife and I faced the added problem that we were evangelical Christians and this is a world where homosexuality finds no place: it is considered to be an abomination. The inference is that gay people have chosen to adopt an unacceptable lifestyle as opposed to a normal lifestyle and the problem is often attributed to inadequate parenting.

In reality, our son was fortunate in having the full support of his brother and sister, as their foreknowledge made it a little easier for him to decide to tell us what he knew would be unwelcome, if not unacceptable, news. According to one lesbian lady with whom we have become friends, coming out to parents is probably the most difficult issue that any homosexual person has to cope with. She is in her mid-fifties and comes from an Irish, Catholic family of ten children. Only three members of her family, two brothers and a sister, are aware that she is lesbian. She had tried to tell her father on one occasion but she is convinced that he had no idea what she was talking about. Perhaps she could not find adequate words and could not face the brutality of being simple and direct.

The difficulty, as she puts it, lies in the fact that coming out to parents is tantamount to saying "*You brought me up and this is how I have turned out.*" It is almost impossible to declare that without implying some blame, and even without blame there is no guarantee of what the response will be. Further, there is the awful burden of knowing that your news will certainly come as a massive disappointment and possibly a great shock if they had never suspected the truth. Many parents of the older generation hold on to traditional family values and prefer to ignore the existence of homosexuality.

The fear of rejection is so great, she says, that words never can adequately convey the feeling to those who have not experienced it for themselves. An insurmountable barrier may form that prevents some people from ever telling their parents and those with religious backgrounds are the most vulnerable in this regard. Sadly, our Irish friend's contact with her family is now very restricted, largely because the chief topic of conversation always seemed to revolve around the issue of when she intended to find a suitable man, get married and have children. Though she is now beyond childbearing age, there still exists the idea of marriage in their minds. Minimal contact with her family seemed an easier option than facing the recurrent awkwardness of having to fend off such thoughtless questions. Nevertheless, she misses her family and wishes that things could be different.

Following our son's revelation, there was a stunned silence. Neither my wife nor I knew how to respond. Life had not prepared us for a moment such as this. It was as if I had switched on the television and been told that a coup had taken place and that the country was now under communist rule, or that Sharia law had been imposed. Somehow I just wasn't able to take it in. I sat there with my brain seemingly disconnected from my vocal cords. In the event that was fortunate, as it prevented me from uttering something on impulse that I may have regretted later. I was conscious only of the fact that the world I had taken for granted for so long had suddenly ceased to exist. With fewer than a dozen words, our son had changed the entire landscape. Though I did not know it at that moment, I had been launched unwillingly on a journey into the unknown, one that would cause me to question and eventually dismantle my most cherished beliefs, ones that had been central to my life for forty years.

In my case, it was not that I was taken completely by surprise by my son's announcement but rather that I was momentarily devastated at having had my worst, suppressed fear confirmed. I say momentarily, because I was guilty of holding the misguided notion that homosexuality was a choice and that sexual preferences could be altered if one was willing. I had never had any reason to question this evangelical

Christian assumption which I knew to be based on Bible teaching.

Although my immediate reaction was one of shock and devastation, it was not too long before I began to take a calmer view. I had just experienced a life-altering moment that may have left me badly injured but I was not mortally wounded. Devastation was soon replaced by determination. I would see my son "healed" and delivered from this perversion. I would never surrender him to the devil. My God was bigger than any of my problems and if he did not approve of homosexual people then surely he would bring deliverance to my son, for all our sakes. Moreover, here was a chance to prove once more that my God was real and was faithful to his promises. It furnished me with the opportunity to update my own testimony in the most dramatic way.

My wife had broken the silence following our son's revelation when she began to cry and she was inconsolable for several minutes. Homophobia is very strong in Peru and homophobic sentiments are often voiced in public. The thought that we ourselves now had a homosexual child was something that she found impossible to take on board. Nobody else spoke and we remained seemingly frozen in time. Goodness knows what my son must have been going through. He had no guarantee of what response he would receive and he was well aware of the evangelical Christian position on the matter.

When I did manage to reconnect with the world, I stood up, went over to him, put my arms around him and told him that he was still my son, that I loved him and that nothing would ever change that fact. I meant every word of what I said, but secretly I was not prepared to accept his statement as being any sort of final word on the matter. I was determined to leave no stone unturned to see him rescued and brought back into the world of "normality". There followed a further awkward silence as we waited for my wife's heart-rending sobs to abate. When they did not, I suggested that the three of them go out together to do their Boxing Day sales-shopping, so that my wife and I could have some time alone to compose ourselves and come to terms with what we had just been told. Our relief at this "get out" was immense, as it probably was for our children who were visibly upset by the obvious distress of their mother.

My wife had been aware of what she referred to as one or two "tell-tale signs" when our son was still quite young and these obviously worried her and she had confided some of her worries to me. She noticed what she thought were occasional, effeminate mannerisms and would gently chide him, reminding him that he was a boy and not a girl. I was not as attuned to these signs as my wife and my concerns did not surface until much later, when the absence of any girlfriends began to make me wonder if her suspicions were more firmly grounded in reality than I wished to admit. We had always hoped, or had chosen to believe, that it was just a case of her being over-sensitive and that he was simply a little different from his older brother and sister. We clung to the hope that one day he would find some girl who would be right for him, that everything would then change and we would all live happily ever after. Perhaps all parents think that kind of thing.

Now, however, those hopes had been dashed and we had been thrust into another, quite different world. I was in a crisis, but one from which I hoped to emerge triumphant with my faith vindicated once and for all. The alternative was something that I could not contemplate at the time: my quest would fail and I would then be obliged to re-evaluate my whole relationship with God and the beliefs that I had held for most of my life.

For evangelicals, and probably for all Christians, faith is more a matter of emotion and personal experience than intellectual conviction. I was not convinced about a number of matters regarding the Bible, ones to which I could find no answer and which had continued, for some time, to be a source of concern. Maybe this would be another opportunity to consolidate my experience of God and hence render the intellectual uncertainties irrelevant.

My wife, of course, was in a similar position. Faith, however, has a personal element to it. Many aspects of faith can be shared with others, but ultimately, you can be sure only of your own journey, and I knew that my response to this crisis was not necessarily going to be the same as my wife's response, even if both of us initially believed that a "cure" was possible. When faith is put on trial, it can reveal differences of belief that are not obvious in the good times.

Our younger son had been a twin, but his twin brother had lived for only two hours. Now my wife, having finally calmed down to the point where she could speak, only managed to say that having lost one of her twins at birth, she had now also lost the other one. Suddenly, he had ceased to be a normal human being in her eyes and was certainly no longer someone who might one day provide her with the grandchildren she so desperately longed for.

Looking back, we were unbelievably self-centred and focussed entirely on our own problems. First, one that faces all parents of gay children: how were we going to tell our families and friends and with whom else could we share this news? Second, how to handle this delicate issue within the church we attended. We were soon to face bigger problems as our marriage was taken to the brink by the strain of the next eighteen months or so.

Initially, my wife was wracked with guilt, blaming herself and wondering what on earth she had done to cause her son to choose homosexuality—and what she might have done to prevent it. At some early stage, however, our other two children managed to convince her that it had nothing to do with his upbringing but was something outside of anyone's control and was not an alterable condition. My own failure to accept that fact was to cause a deepening rift between us.

The truth is that neither of us knew anything about homosexuality apart from several references in the Bible, all of which condemned it. Hence, we did not properly appreciate the full force of his words, which were "*I'm gay*" ["I **AM** gay"]. What I, at least, heard was "*I have **chosen** to follow a gay lifestyle*," because that is how evangelical Christianity insists on regarding it. With hindsight, I am appalled and ashamed that I could ever have been so ignorant. I can only guess at the stress that our son must have suffered as he struggled to come to terms with his sexuality during adolescence, compounded by the fact that he knew that being gay might well cause estrangement from us, his religious parents. At the time that he would have had most need of us, we were not available to him. The knowledge of this fact still causes a deep and unremitting hurt within me.

There are many issues that will be common to all parents of gay children, regardless of any particular beliefs that they may have. I cannot imagine any heterosexual parent wishing to have a homosexual child, because this takes them into a world beyond their own immediate experience and hence one with which they will find it hard to identify. I am certain that the vast majority of parents will struggle with the issue of their own coming out to their families and friends. It is not as easy to remain as quiet about such things as one might like. We have friends who constantly ask us if our children have "*found anybody yet*" and whether they may be getting married and giving us grandchildren anytime soon. It is the same kind of question that the Irish lady I mentioned earlier constantly had to fend off. You do not mind when your children are heterosexual. It is surprisingly difficult to come up with an answer when the child concerned is gay. Whether we like it or not, many people are judgemental and parents have a natural instinct to protect their offspring. Nevertheless, their child's world is one that they will need to come to terms with if they wish to maintain any meaningful relationship with him or her.

I understand my elder son because, in general, I can identify with his desires and I have an image of some kind of future where his life is concerned. That future features marriage and children, even though these things may never happen. I have a similar vision of the future for my daughter that makes sense to my understanding of how things in the world are ordered and where most people find happiness and fulfilment.

The kind of future that faces my gay son, however, is much harder for me to envisage. I know that he will face some prejudice, not least from those claiming to represent the God who they say "*so loves the world.*" This would not be such a problem if these prejudiced people were obviously bad or clearly deluded. It is a problem because, by and large, they are very respectable and pleasant. They do a great deal of good and their leaders are generally held in high regard and their views given significant credence, even if their influence has declined over recent years.

My own difficulties were compounded by my being part of the specifically evangelical Christian world. Just how I came to be a part of this world, and why I deemed the beliefs that I had sufficiently credible to hold them for so long, needs a little explanation. To understand a journey, it is necessary to know why the journey had to be made in the first place and the specific reasons that caused the journey to take the path that ended where it did. That will involve recalling some wonderful times, as well as some rather less wonderful ones, spent in Uganda and then Peru. But first, I must say a little about my own upbringing.

Chapter 2   EVANGELICAL CHRISTIANITY

To my knowledge, there is no agreed definition of the word evangelical. I use it to signify people who believe that the Bible is a divinely inspired book with absolute authority in all matters of faith and conduct and who base their beliefs on its teachings. Great emphasis is placed on people having a life-transforming, personal faith in Jesus, something which is accompanied by the guaranteed assurance of an eternity in heaven. Faith is the central, motivating factor in their lives, not some convenient add-on or insurance policy.

Historically, it refers to people involved in the religious awakenings of the eighteenth century and later, and was strongly associated with social reform. William Wilberforce was a prominent evangelical, famous for his crusade to abolish the transatlantic slave trade. While social concern is still part of the evangelical world, the emphasis that it once had has probably diminished a little over time.

Nevertheless, at the heart of evangelical Christianity there is an immensely powerful message. It is of a God who loves you, so much so that he sent his Son to die in order to purchase your forgiveness. He loves you enough to come and share your life and empower you to be an overcomer in all of life's circumstances. To experience God's love enables you to "*have life, and have it to the full*" in the here and now (John 10:10). The only thing required on your part is to accept all of this, to be willing to allow God to have his way and acknowledge that it has all been made possible through Jesus Christ and his sacrificial death on your behalf.

Love is one of the greatest needs in the life of any human being, and for most people it is an essential ingredient for happiness. To know that you are loved unconditionally is, without doubt, a glorious feeling and one that enables you to live on a higher plane. It is not something to be lightly despised, even if, at the end of the day, it may be an illusion.

Evangelicals believe in the divine inspiration of the Bible, a concept that does leave some room for manoeuvre; for the inclusion of a mythical element when this serves to illustrate some important truth. Beyond this, there are those who believe in the literal truth of every single word in the Bible. In the English speaking world, this usually means every word of the King James translation. Such people are known as fundamentalists and their number appears to be growing quite quickly.

The advantage of holding fundamentalist beliefs is that they offer certainty, and we live in a world where most people value certainty over truth. We want answers and will follow those who claim that they have these answers. Conviction, right or wrong, seems to be more attractive and reassuring than any alternative. Fundamentalism also removes the need to decide where the boundary might lie between fact and myth. The downside of fundamentalism is its rigidity, its incapacity to accommodate new knowledge. The creation story is literal truth, so evolution is not only wrong, it must be an invention of the devil.

In the USA, over the last forty years, this movement has become closely identified with extreme right wing politics and its ideas have been increasingly adopted by the Republican Party, aware of the huge potential this represents at the ballot box. Leaders such as the late Jerry Falwell, a Baptist pastor and founder of the Moral Majority, and Pat Robertson, made (in Pat Robertson's case, still make) no secret of their desire for fundamentalist Christian opinion to exert as much influence as possible over political decision making.

Because there is an inevitable tendency for all new movements to lose some of their initial fervour, there always exists a periodic need for renewal. Fundamentalists, on the extreme edge of the evangelical movement, regarded themselves as the product of one such renewal and then, inevitably, tended to view themselves as the only true believers. Like their Islamic counterparts, their leaders are most likely to be male and authoritarian, rigid in their beliefs and hence unable to cope with differences of opinion. There are, thankfully, a small number of notable exceptions to this generalised description.

Salvation is regarded as a "done deed" in the evangelical world, and there is a belief in "*once saved, always saved.*" It is usual, therefore, to claim that those who come to reject what they had apparently once believed about the Christian faith were never "really saved" in the first place. There is no room for the idea that people may have a genuine change of mind as they learn more and understand more about the beliefs to which they have committed themselves. To express doubt is often sufficient to relegate you to the realm of outcast. To change your mind is to become a traitor, worthy of every possible condemnation. No properly saved person would ever question any of the beliefs that they originally accepted.

I write what follows, therefore, to show that my own credentials as a saved person were perfectly legitimate, and yet despite this, and passionate as I once was in my beliefs, I did come to change my mind. The change occurred, not because I wanted to belong to "the world" and was no longer willing to pay the price of discipleship, or even because belief was no longer convenient now that I had a gay child. It was simply because I dared to engage in an honest search for the truth and confront the doubts that I harboured, doubts that centred on claims that the Bible was the infallible, divinely inspired, Word of God.

The family that I was born into was not particularly religious. My father was in favour of religion provided that he himself did not have to be involved. He seemed to think that it was good for others and particularly for his own children; or perhaps he felt it would be good for his own image if his children were seen to be having a Christian upbringing. The children of respectable families attended church and my father certainly considered himself to be respectable.

My mother came from an intensely religious Catholic family, but she rebelled and married outside the Catholic faith. She was the second child in a large family, growing up mainly during the 1920s and 30s, and like many other families at that time, they struggled to make ends meet. There were eventually fourteen children, although the eldest, a boy, had died in infancy before my mother was born and three more boys were to die before reaching their teenage years. My mother, the second child, thus became the eldest of ten surviving children. She herself was sent out to do baby-sitting as soon as she was old enough to cope with such responsibility, in order to help with family finances. My grandfather was a coalminer but there was no guarantee of continuous employment.

My mother's objections to the Roman Catholic Church revolved around two issues. One of these was the fact that, despite the family's obvious poverty, at least one local Irish clergyman made efforts to solicit funds for the IRA during regular pastoral visits. As it happens, my grandfather, who was born and raised in what is now the Republic of Ireland, appears to have had little time for the IRA or any of its supporters, and had serious misgivings regarding people who lived in England and yet sought to bite the hand that fed them.

The second issue was concerned with childbearing. One visiting clergyman, possibly the same one just mentioned, clearly thought that it was the duty of every Catholic family to have as many children as possible. Unexplained pauses in the process of childbearing were viewed with some concern, both by himself and the Church. A pause had occurred during a period when my grandmother had suffered from a rather protracted illness whose cause was never established. My mother must have been present on one occasion when this subject was broached and she certainly, in later life, held the opinion that uncontrolled childbearing was a prime cause of the poverty in which her family had been entrenched. She never forgot these incidents and nursed her resentment against what she considered to be the Church's unwarranted interference in politics and family matters for the rest of her life.

Despite all of this, she did appear to maintain some faith in God. When my brothers and I reached school age, we were sent to the local primary school, which, as it happened, was a faith-based Anglican school, the building doubling up as a church on Sundays. It appears that at least one parent was expected to attend church services and my mother dutifully took up this obligation. Children were also encouraged to attend the Sunday school, and it was in this environment that I received my early Christian education, absorbing the stories of Jesus and well-known Old Testament figures such as Abraham, Moses, Elijah, Samson and King David, to name the ones that I remember the best.

All this clearly had an effect on me because at a later age I carried on with church attendance from choice. While I was often bored by the liturgy, I was all ears when it came to the sermon. We had one or two particularly good visiting preachers and one excellent curate when I was a teenager. The curate was also interested in football, a passion of mine, and so I was hooked.

It was not until I went to university, however, that I had any contact with evangelical Christianity. It was here that I encountered Christians for whom religion was not just an interest but was an all-consuming passion. Until that point, my own version of the faith had consisted in little more than the idea of "being good" in order that I might one day go to heaven. These evangelicals seemed to know that their names were already written in heaven. They were "saved": Jesus was a living presence in their lives and he was the great motivator behind everything that they did. Being saved was such a fantastic experience that they were driven to try and share it with anybody and everybody who would listen. They had a purpose about them which I lacked. I was impressed and it did not take long for me to realise that this was something that I also wanted to have: it appeared to be the answer to some deep longing that existed within me.

The evangelical Christians with whom I associated at university were some of the most wonderful people that I have ever had the privilege to meet. Most were committed, loving and generous, with high ideals and a desire to "do good" and make the world a better place. Central to accomplishing this was the need to convert as many people as possible to have a belief in Jesus. This emphasis has probably replaced some of the earlier emphasis on social work, or at least has more tightly entwined social action with evangelistic endeavour. My whole experience of evangelical Christianity over forty years was mostly positive, and I do not wish to imply in anything that follows that these people are, in many ways, anything other than the "salt of the earth" that they believe themselves to be.

Problems arise, however, if your beliefs are not necessarily correct, and you ascribe unchallengeable authority to a book on the grounds that you believe it to be inspired. When this is coupled with the belief that the Holy Spirit guides your interpretation of what is written in this book, it can lead even the most well-intentioned people to adopt attitudes that are not only uncharitable but are unacceptable when they arise from beliefs that are in conflict with modern knowledge and scientific opinion. Also, there can be a considerable amount of self-righteousness involved when people maintain their prerogative to hold certain views regardless of the consequences for others.

My induction into the world of evangelical Christianity contained what was to me a very strange element at the time: I needed to accept that the Bible was the inspired Word of God, an inerrant guide in all matters of faith and conduct. I say "strange" because I was being asked to accept this when there were still large parts of the Bible that I had never read. I accepted the proposition, not out of conviction, but because this is what they believed and I wanted to be one of them.

Personal influence plays a major part in most decisions to join a movement and personal relationships are among the strongest reasons why people continue to be members, especially so in the early stages of membership. This was certainly true in my case. What I did not realise at the time was the inevitable consequence of accepting a proposition which stands in complete contrast to the scientific culture of our age. It says, in effect, that if you want to be a real Christian, you cannot subject your faith to the normal processes of reason or require evidence for your beliefs. Faith is, by its very essence, unquestioning belief. Lack of faith is seen as a deliberate choice to question, or doubt, the Word of God, and hence cuts you off from all the blessings of God. It is a self-protecting system and a highly effective one.

University provided me with a wonderful opportunity to become acquainted with Christians from different denominations and to attend different churches. It was here that I first encountered the Pentecostal movement with its emphasis on an experience known as the "Baptism with the Holy Spirit" accompanied by "speaking in tongues". Other gifts of the Spirit may also be bestowed on the believer, the gift of healing being the most prominent or highly prized. However, a more modern attitude places greater emphasis on healing as a biblical promise for every believer rather than a gift bestowed upon the few.

Healing began to gain huge prominence in the second half of the twentieth century. Prayer for healing, with the genuine expectation that the sick would be healed, had been a feature of Pentecostal church services since they started, at the beginning of last century. I had experience of this Pentecostal belief in healing while in my final year at university. I had always been plagued with a rather bad stammer and someone I met in the university Christian Union suggested that I attend a Pentecostal church service with him. Prayer for healing in a Pentecostal church was the answer to my problem he assured me.

At the end of the service that we attended, as I was leaving, the pastor shook hands with me and asked me if I was saved. It was only the second time that I had been asked this question. The other occasion was my initial contact with evangelical Christians in my first week at university. I must have stuttered in my reply because he suggested that I return the following week and the church would pray for my healing. This they did. Nothing dramatic happened as a result, but the following week, before the service began, the pastor approached me and asked me to do one of the Bible readings. I must admit that I was petrified and the chosen passage, a Psalm, seemed to me to be very long. However, I read without faltering, the first time in my life that I had ever managed such a feat.

One of my greatest dreads at school was caused by having to take my turn at reading in English classes, or reciting the poetry that we had had to learn for homework. Part of the purpose of this was to inculcate confidence in using the voice in front of an audience, but it was always a dreadful ordeal for me and also for the rest of the class whenever I was required to speak. Gradually, after my experience with this Pentecostal church, my speech did get better and somewhere along the line my stammer virtually disappeared and now is only an occasional problem, usually if I am particularly tired or stressed.

Healing crusades grew out of this emphasis on healing and they became more common in the second half of the twentieth century. The fascination with healing is partly driven by the desperation to provide some cast-iron proof that Christianity is "the truth". A God who heals is a God who exists. One genuine healing would be worth ten thousand words of persuasive argument. After all, Jesus apparently authenticated his own ministry by means of miraculous signs.

Many of the evangelists who engage in healing crusades passionately believe in what they preach and engage in this sort of ministry out of a genuine desire to bring all the blessings of the Gospel, as they see it, to a very needy world. All such ministries, however, have huge problems associated with them. One particular need is that of generating faith in the hearers. Even Jesus is said to have been unable to do any mighty works in his home town of Nazareth on account of the unbelief of the people there (Mark 6:5; Matt 13:58). The temptation to exaggerate in order to try and produce the faith necessary to receive healing is, under the circumstances, enormous.

Some evangelists get carried away by the atmosphere they create and wild claims are often made in efforts to generate faith, so that it is difficult to know where reality ends and hype begins. If this is the case today, we cannot discount the fact that early believers, and the Gospel writers, would have been subject to all the same temptations to exaggeration when the Gospel was taking root.

Beyond the ministries that have resulted from a genuine belief that God does still heal today, there are inevitably the charlatans who see the prospect of "*gold in them thar ills*" as somebody once said. In a recent Channel 4 television documentary, *Miracles for Sale*, Derren Brown exposed some of the techniques used by a number of evangelists to fabricate healings in order to generate faith. It all makes for a disturbing scenario.

A big question does revolve around the issue of whether there is any firm evidence that any of these evangelists perform any genuine healings, no matter how sincere their motives may be. I can only say that I have attended a number of healing crusades in my time and I harbour many misgivings about them. I cannot say for certain whether any genuinely miraculous healings occur, but they certainly do not do so in any significant number and I, personally, have never witnessed anything that I would describe as a major miracle. There is no doubt at all that the success rates in healing ministries are negligible when compared to the healings achieved through conventional medicine.

There is one overriding issue with healing today that would not have arisen in Bible times. There are some pastors and evangelists with healing ministries who say that in order to be healed people must have faith in the God who heals and not in anything else. You cannot expect God to heal you while your faith is placed in the medical treatment you are receiving. Medication must therefore be thrown away along with any other crutch, such as wearing spectacles, before healing can be expected from God. The dangers involved in doing this cannot be overstated. In the time of Jesus, faith may have been the only option. Today's alternative of modern medical treatment places some believers in a considerable quandary.

As the teachings of the Pentecostal Church filtered into the established denominational churches, they gave rise to what became known as the charismatic movement. Tensions then often arose between the new "Spirit-filled" or charismatic believers and the more traditional believers. Many charismatic Christians, frustrated by what they saw as resistance to this "*new move of the Spirit*," left their denominations and banded together with other dissatisfied charismatics from different churches to form independent fellowships. A large number of these have now grown into very successful churches in their own right. I have been a member of more than one charismatic church during my lifetime.

Over the years I have observed many different emphases in teaching even within a particular church. There is, without question, a tendency to chase after what is new or fashionable among many believers. It is customary to defend this approach by claiming it is to do with "*what God (or the Holy Spirit) is teaching the Church today.*" A lot of this has been fuelled by the revolution in communication technology. What is happening in one part of the world now becomes common knowledge almost everywhere within a very short space of time so that it has become much easier to keep abreast of what "God is doing", or what he is supposedly doing.

Prophecy is another issue that has grown in prominence in recent years and it received a considerable boost when the State of Israel was established in 1948, apparently fulfilling some Old Testament prophecies. This event gave rise to renewed interest in End Time theology, particularly with regard to the fortunes of the Jews and the land of Israel prior to the Second Coming of Jesus. Hal Lindsay's book on the subject, *The Late Great Planet Earth*, published in 1970, became a huge success, and still seems to be read.

The origins of Zionism go much further back than 1948 and are very well documented in Victoria Clark's excellent book *Allies for Armageddon: The Rise of Christian Zionism*. The rationale behind much of the present day Christian Zionism can be attributed to a verse in Genesis 12:3 where God says to Abraham: "*I will bless those who bless you, and whoever curses you I will curse.*" Desperate for the blessings of God, American fundamentalist Christians in particular pour millions of dollars into supporting the nation of Israel and its claims to the whole land of Palestine and often much besides. The fear, emphasised by some fund-raising ministers who focus on this aspect of the Gospel, is that if America ceases to bless Israel, God will cease to bless America. The Palestinians, as a group of people, are rather unfortunate victims in all of this as the Bible fails to mention them in the overall scheme of things. Hence neither they nor their welfare are of any consequence in the minds of many fundamentalist Christians.

Another hugely important facet of prophecy is that Jesus appeared to fulfil a number of Old Testament prophecies, particularly those found in Psalm 22 and Isaiah chapter 53. These, along with other prophecies, are put forward as the conclusive proof that Jesus is the Son of God and the Saviour of the world.

One last major trend worth mentioning has been the tendency to embrace the "prosperity" gospel. This emphasises the goodness of God and his desire to bless all believers in every conceivable way. So God wants everybody to partake of the rich and abundant blessings that he so liberally supplies, spiritual, material and in all matters of health. Believers are encouraged to learn all the promises that are contained in the Bible that pertain to health, wealth and spiritual well-being and to claim these promises for themselves. There is no doubt a great deal of value in this approach because it does increase faith and faith can produce a feeling of wellbeing which, in all probability, will lead to greater happiness and better health. It is certainly a very attractive message and this explains why it has made considerable gains in popularity since its "discovery" in the USA. It does, however, tend to ignore other parts of the Bible that one might describe as rather less desirable, such as the exhortation of Jesus to deny ourselves, take up the cross and follow him.

Nevertheless, there is an undeniable and life-transforming power in the evangelical message.

Coupled with the certainty that it offers, I do not wonder that I was hooked on it for so long. I would even say that I was far happier when I could believe in its truth than I am today. Then again, I am not a homosexual. If I had been, I might have realised that the Gospel is not quite as all-embracing as some people would like to believe. It appears to be restricted to those who are able to fit into its template. Since there is no reliable evidence to suggest that a change of sexual orientation is possible, Christianity has nothing to say to homosexuals except to tell them that they are not welcome in the kingdom of heaven. It was this realisation that made me begin to question the truth of what I had believed for so long.

Chapter 3   UGANDA

Before finishing university I had already decided that I wanted to be a missionary. As funds for most English missionary societies were in short supply at that time, there was a major effort in university Christian Union societies to encourage people to take up overseas contracts in the secular sector, thereby funding themselves. Teaching was particularly targeted, as this job involved working directly with "the future" and was seen as a job which would offer more opportunities in terms of time and immediate access to people.

As a result, I applied to the Ministry of Overseas Development (as it then was) to go on a Diploma in Education (now called PGCE) course at Makerere University in Kampala, Uganda. Part of the agreement was that we would do at least two years teaching in an East African school following successful completion of the course. In the event, teaching in East Africa turned out to be so pleasant that most people stayed considerably longer than the minimum two years required. Contracts could be renewed as often as people wished, with a generous period of leave allowed between successive contracts.

It was in Uganda that I really did become aware of the power of the Gospel to change people's lives. Uganda, Kenya and probably most other parts of Africa, had huge problems resulting from poverty, a genuine lack of opportunity for many, and a lack of anything that could be construed as entertainment for most. Drinking filled this vacuum in many cases. In the local villages, the drinking was done with people sitting around a communal pot which contained a fermenting liquid (a traditional alcoholic beverage known locally as pombe) which was frequently topped-up with hot water. Several long, thin tubes were placed into this pot to act as straws, and these would be passed from person to person, each one taking a sip before passing the tube along.

This particular form of drinking posed several problems: first there was no control over the strength of the fermenting liquid or "beer"; second no one had any idea of just how much they had drunk; third, the liquid would go on fermenting while in the stomach. The result was that almost everybody would end up the worse for wear, several would be very much the worse for wear, and a few would become violent. Women were often on the receiving end of this violence.

One such woman arrived at my house one day with two children, a girl aged about eight or nine and a boy aged five or six. At that time, few in Uganda had any clear idea of when they had been born and hence of exactly how old they were. The woman herself had an arm that was clearly broken, the result of having been beaten with a stick by her husband, probably following one such afternoon drinking session. As a result she was temporarily incapable of looking after her children.

The girl had been crippled by polio and could not walk; she dragged herself along the floor on her hands and knees. Her knees were swollen, misshapen and always dirty as a result of doing this. It was particularly tragic because vaccinations against polio were available in local hospitals. Information, however, did not always reach the outlying villages and even when it did, parents had to make the effort to take their children to hospital. A round trip of over twenty miles is a long way, particularly if it involves walking along dusty paths in hot sunshine, and it becomes a less attractive proposition when the dangers of a disease or the benefits of the vaccination are not fully understood.

The boy had a particularly bad chest infection. Both of these children stayed with my "houseboy", the general term used in those days for a man employed as a domestic help. He also happened to be their uncle and lived in accommodation attached to the house. His village home was too far away to travel to and fro each day and so he would go there for weekends only. Ironically, he had also been a victim of polio when young and he hopped around on one leg most of the time, using a home-made crutch to move any distance.

The boy's problem was easily cured with antibiotics from the local hospital and he returned to his village after a short stay and when his mother was able to resume looking after him. The girl stayed for several months, after which she was able to transfer to a Leprosy Mission hospital about 40 miles (64 km) away. There, she was treated by Dutch doctors and given muscle transplant surgery followed by physiotherapy. By the time they had finished with her, she was able to walk upright, although one of her legs needed an iron support. However, some years after I had left Uganda, I learned that she had eventually been able to marry and have children—something which, I suspect, would have been impossible without the treatment.

The traditional alcoholic drink was often used as a substitute for food, and when this occurred it inevitably interfered with people's ability to fulfil their duties in the workplace. This was particularly true of one or two of the African teaching staff in the school where I worked. Admittedly, a number of these staff had not only been forced into teaching against their wishes but had then been placed in a school outside their own tribal area. Under such circumstances, their general lack of motivation, coupled with the tendency to seek solace in alcohol, was hardly surprising.

Evangelical Christianity proved to be a highly effective antidote to this problem. The "saved" ones did not drink. They stopped beating their wives. They became more responsible in looking after their children and in making sure they had clothes and food, went to school and had the required vaccinations. In effect, they became model citizens, acquiring what was called the protestant work ethic and also the invaluable characteristics of reliability and honesty.

Thus, evangelical Christianity was much more of a force for good in Uganda than I had ever been aware of in England, probably because there were more obvious opportunities to make a difference. Also there was little competition. Help, other than basic medical help if you were fortunate enough to live close to one of the major towns, was practically non-existent outside of religious organisations. Major towns were typically more than fifty miles apart, putting effective medical assistance from the state beyond the reach of many. The existence of medical mission hospitals and the local health initiatives that these hospitals often encouraged were therefore of no small value to significant numbers of the population.

Uganda was fortunate to have some wonderful evangelical preachers whose influence for good was immense. At the time, the best known of these was Festo Kivengere, later to be a bishop. One of the great privileges of going to Uganda was that it gave me not only a number of opportunities of hearing this great man preach, but also of meeting him and even sharing a lunch table with him on occasion. He was always extremely friendly, courteous and obliging. He was both an extremely gifted evangelist and also the most ordinary of men at the same time. I was hugely influenced by his great faith and warm personality, but most particularly by his ability to portray the experience of salvation in such thrilling terms and his Jesus-like ability to present deep truths in simple, memorable stories. His untimely death from leukaemia at the age of 60 was a great loss to the world as well as to Uganda.

Another wonderful person who I was also privileged to meet was Archbishop Janani Luwum who was murdered in 1977 for his open opposition to Idi Amin's government. The influence of such people lived on, however, as I was subsequently to find out.

In Uganda I also met a world of witchcraft, demons and supposedly bewitched or demon-possessed people. They were generally, though not always, among the less educated and poorer village people. This is, perhaps, not so surprising, as demons, evil spirits and magic were part and parcel of the world in which they lived. There were some gifted African preachers who formed their own independent churches and who made a big thing of demonic possession and the "casting-out" of demons. I witnessed a number of these occurrences, but I was never persuaded that they were authentic. Perhaps I was just a sceptic at heart, but that, of course, is what much of my education had taught me to be.

Towards the end of my time in Uganda, the school had a vibrant Christian union with about thirty to forty members being drawn from the sixth form, a number of whom had obvious leadership potential. Holiday Christian conferences for students had been quite common for a long time. Initially these had been largely the domain of Scripture Union, but their conferences were rather staid and presented a very English version of Christianity. However, from the early 1970s, a number of young, gifted, African evangelists had begun organising their own conferences and these were much more popular. They had dared to throw off the missionary yolk and they made religion exciting and the Gospel message relevant to the daily lives of modern young Africans.

It was in this environment that I was introduced to a whole new experience of worship. These leaders would shout to their audiences: *"We Africans cannot worship with a hymn-book in our hands. The Bible tells us to lift up our hands to the sanctuary and praise the Lord* (Psalm 134:2). *It tells us to praise his name with dancing and make music to him with tambourine and harp* (Psalm 149:3). *We Africans love to make music and we love to dance. Let us make music and dance for our God"*

Simple choruses that encapsulated the essence of the Gospel message were set to catchy tunes with strong, rhythmic music. Other choruses would have haunting melodies. Many such choruses could be sung not only in English but also in all the different tribal languages. One chorus, sung in different languages, could easily last for twenty minutes. The effect of two or three hundred people singing and engaging in rhythmic dancing could be hypnotic. It was easy to imagine yourself being transported from the often mundane routine of life into the heavens and the very presence of God. Worship became a thrilling experience. Similar worship has now become commonplace in a number of the new, independent, charismatic churches in the English speaking world, but I have never known anywhere else that has quite captured the magical atmosphere of these meetings in East Africa.

Coupled with this was a huge enthusiasm to bring the kingdom of God down to earth and establish it in their midst. These preachers nailed their colours to the mast. Biblical standards were to prevail. There was to be a complete break with many traditional African customs. Drinking and smoking were taboo as was sex outside of marriage. Living God's way was in. They preached with contagious enthusiasm. The kingdom of God was an exciting place to be and young people were being drawn to it in large numbers.

Most of these conferences had been held in Kenya or major cities in Uganda but none had ever been staged in my own particular region, some two hundred and twenty miles upcountry from the capital, Kampala. Conferences in Uganda, however, had begun to dry up as the general situation there deteriorated under the dictatorship of Idi Amin. As a result, we decided to try and organise a conference of our own, at our school, for the whole of Uganda, although we realised that distance would be a limiting factor on the feasibility of attendance.

Nearly forty years later, I cannot remember clearly a lot of the details of this conference, only the broad outline. We had planned to finance the conference ourselves as far as possible so that students would only have to find fees for transport and not for their food or accommodation. It was possible to feed large numbers of students in Africa for a small fraction of the cost that would be involved in England. Also, the school allowed us to have the accommodation free and even provided the catering staff, provided we pay the cooks. The school was a large boarding school that normally housed about nine hundred boys, somewhat more than its intended capacity. We were hoping to attract anything in excess of a hundred students, and in the end about two hundred and fifty attended.

It was a large and ambitious undertaking, given that none of us had any previous experience of organising any sort of conference. We were simply excited to be doing God's work and believed that he would provide for all our needs. Nevertheless, we were fully aware that things could go badly wrong and so we began regular prayer meetings to make sure, as far as possible, that we had the blessing of God in all that we were trying to do. Indeed, such was the commitment of the students that many of them gave up their lunch time (and lunch!) to pray in the small chapel that the school had, continuing this on a number of days each week for several weeks.

There were three major concerns that I can clearly remember. One was that we would attract enough students to make the conference viable: just getting information to other schools and hence to the students was difficult enough. A second and very major problem concerned the provision of food for the students that did come. The third problem that arose, late on, was the matter of a conference speaker, as we unfortunately lost contact with our original choice for this role.

All these conferences had one great attraction apart from any religious significance. Most African boarding schools were single sex. The conferences were mixed and hence provided an opportunity for young people to be in an environment with members of the opposite sex of their own age. You cannot fight this natural desire so you might as well try and use it to your advantage. Education and the common language (English) that it provided had begun to enable many young people to cross traditional tribal barriers. These young people belonged to a much bigger and a much more exciting world than that of their parents. Village life and arranged marriages were no longer part of their vision. School and education had provided them with new horizons and they had discovered something of the joys of freedom. Part of this involved the freedom to find love for themselves.

No religion can be divorced from the realities of life. African preachers fearlessly engaged with the interests of young people. They talked about relationships, sex, responsibility and self-control, and the joys of a Christian marriage. This meant one man with one wife. It was a particularly attractive vision for the girls, but the idea was sold to the boys with equal success. They were given a new vision for the future and many of them wanted to share that future with others of like mind. The student Christian conferences provided a marvellous forum in which young people could explore these new ideas and opportunities in the company of others all with similar interests. Despite Uganda's many difficulties, there was a more than a reasonable chance that, providing news of our conference could be got around, people would come.

The problem of food became increasingly acute as time went by and food in the country at large became ever more scarce because of the collapse in the economy and general infrastructure of the country. Even when food was plentiful, transport for moving it around the country was in very short supply. The problem of getting food to schools reached such a level that the school holidays throughout the country were suddenly brought forward by two weeks to give a little more breathing space to the beleaguered minister responsible for these matters.

The change in the holiday dates meant that our conference would now be held in the last week of the school holidays instead of the first week. The day after the students departed for home, a delivery of food, intended for the town in general and our school in particular, arrived unexpectedly at a local, privately owned store. As fortune would have it, I happened to be in the town and in the vicinity of the store at the moment the delivery arrived. Our school was situated nearly five miles, or half an hour's bicycle ride, outside the town and I cannot remember just why I had made the visit that particular day.

Nevertheless, I now found myself at a store with a storekeeper willing to sell me as much food as I wanted, given that I could pay cash and would pay up-front. This was in contrast to the school, which had an account with the store but settled its bills in arrears, probably seriously in arrears in many cases. Consequently, I was able to buy food to feed about four hundred people for four days, knowing that I could sell any surplus to the school afterwards. Our first miracle in answer to all of our prayers had just been received!

Immediately after this, I had to travel to Nairobi, Kenya, to get my car serviced, as reliable servicing facilities in Uganda had ceased to exist. I also wanted to see if I could persuade any of the Christian friends that I had made in Nairobi to come and help us at our conference and, in particular, to see if I could find someone to shoulder the responsibility of being principal speaker.

Africans in general, and the friends that I had made in particular, were exceptionally hospitable. It was always possible to turn up unannounced, almost at any time, and be given food and lodging. This was fortunate because it was usually impossible to give any prior warning of a visit in those days. In the house where I stayed on this occasion, the main topic of conversation concerned a Manasseh Mankuleiyo and his co-worker, Margaret Wangari. Manasseh was a young Masai preacher who was making a name for himself in Nairobi. Margaret seemed to have a special healing gift and she prayed for the sick at the end of each meeting. I was taken to attend one of his weekend meetings, which I can still remember quite well. It was held in some open, grassy area somewhere in Nairobi and there were what I estimated to be several thousand people in attendance, although I seemed to be the only white person present.

Manasseh turned out to be an engaging young man who spoke from a small, raised, wooden platform, large enough for him and a band of about four musicians together with some amplifiers that were operated from car batteries. He spoke with confidence and without any of the theatrics often used by open-air preachers. He talked about the privilege and joy of knowing Jesus as a personal friend, of having God on your side as you walked through life, of the joy of having your sins forgiven and your name written in heaven and the wonderful experience of belonging to the "new community", the "kingdom of God" on earth. I could not help comparing this, in my mind, with another preacher, two thousand years earlier, who probably operated in similar circumstances except for the electronics.

People who have steady jobs with guaranteed salaries and secure futures cannot always appreciate the attraction of having a God to walk beside you in the daily struggle of life. For those who have no guarantee of being able to feed their families at the end of each day, hearing this message could be akin to finding a pearl of great price.

At the end of the meeting, Margaret prayed for the sick, though not using the platform as it was too small. It was impossible to see what was happening as I was somewhere at the back, although there were occasional shouts of joy and afterwards I noticed several crutches lying abandoned on the grass. There was certainly an atmosphere of great happiness that pervaded the whole gathering and it was easy to see why they were attracting such a large following.

I recall being fortunate enough to have the opportunity to speak to Manasseh at the end of the event. I told him how much I had enjoyed his meeting and explained who I was and what we were trying to do in Uganda, whose difficulties under Idi Amin were well known by this time. I also told him that problems beyond our control had left us without a speaker and I asked if he could possibly come and help us. He must have asked to meet me to discuss the matter further, because I remember sitting in a café with him the next day where, to my huge amazement but great delight, he said that he would love to help and that he would bring Margaret with him. Here was another "miraculous" answer to prayer, one beyond my wildest dreams.

Promises to help, and the promised help actually materialising, however, were not always the same thing. Sometimes people would make promises with the best of intentions and yet not be able to keep their word because of circumstance beyond their control. It is so much easier to plan with certainty in a country such as England, unless, of course, your plans depend upon having good weather. So, when I got back to Uganda with my news, we knew that this was only half the battle. An African Christian friend on the staff and I, together with a small group of students who returned to the school a few days early to help with final arrangements, prayed with some fervour that nothing would impede Manasseh and Margaret from attending, though I must admit that there was some acute anxiety on my part. I did not dare contemplate what would happen if our guests failed to show up. I might have ended up being the main speaker myself and the conference would have been a disaster. In fact, I might not have been alive to tell the tale. African students could be rather unpredictable if they felt cheated.

It was not only Manasseh and Margaret that we needed. We also needed some students and we had no idea how many (if any!) to expect. So, when the big day arrived and students started to materialise, our spirits began to soar. When our guest speaker and his co-worker also arrived, having travelled a distance of three hundred and thirty miles, including a border crossing, we could only marvel at the mighty God that we served. By evening, when the first meeting was held, there were two hundred and fifty students, male and female, present in approximately equal numbers. I cannot remember exactly what arrangements we made for the girls because ours was a boys' school and there were no dedicated facilities for females. We must have managed somehow because I cannot remember any problems arising.

The conference, to my great relief, ran very smoothly, although I was kept busy and I did not manage to attend all of the daytime meetings. Such was the thirst for the "Word of God" that we simply ran four two-hour meetings each day, one after a morning cup of tea but before breakfast, one between breakfast and lunch, one in the afternoon and one in the evening. There was such enthusiasm at these gatherings that it was never necessary to provide alternative "entertainment", something common at the English-run Scripture Union camps where religion seemed to something of an add-on. Perhaps it is true that religion flourishes best in times of hardship and uncertainty, and Uganda had no shortage of either of these.

I do not remember any great miracles happening. We certainly had no blind students in attendance but we did have one of our own school students who had been crippled in both legs by polio. He used a wheelchair to get around and he was still using his wheelchair at the end of the conference. Mostly, the need seemed to be that of relief from headaches or toothache, and, in the case of girls, period pains. These may not seem to be life-threatening issues but for people who often had no ready access to the most basic medicines they were real and important enough.

I do recall that I, and all of our school students who attended the conference, lived in a state of considerable exhilaration for several weeks after the conference had ended. Indeed, from this time on, our regular meetings were infused with passion: we shared together, prayed with fervour and worshipped with abandon. Despite the absence of nearly all things material, we were deliriously happy. It was experiences such as these that gave me, at the time, a certainty that my God was real and I cannot recall ever being able to recapture what I considered to be such moments of joy in the presence of God once I had left Uganda.

Nevertheless, I knew that I had still had much to learn. The issues of healing and the miraculous, in particular, were ones that would not go away. My experiences in these areas had been somewhat mixed. At best they were inconclusive and at worst rather confusing. A particular area of concern was to be one that possibly sowed the first seeds of doubt into my mind.

Towards the end of my first three-year sojourn in Uganda, I had fallen ill with a rather bad dose of malaria. The first twenty-four hours were a grim experience: high fever, constant vomiting, diarrhoea, a bad headache and a severe pain across my back. I think that I just wanted to die at the time, despite the fact that, as an overseas contracted worker, I had access to special privileges. I was provided with a bed in a separate room immediately on my arrival at the hospital, given a blood test to confirm the illness, seen by a doctor and given treatment.

It should not be imagined that the facilities were in any way equivalent to our own National Health Service, however. The toilet was down a corridor and was of typical African design in those days, being situated at ground level, although it had a flushing system. To use it required squatting down and balancing over the hole, a particularly difficult task when you are also feeling sick and dizzy, and it was made considerably more tricky by the need to fend off further attacks from mosquitoes. I visited this venue on several occasions during the first day. I would invariably vomit into a bowl when I crawled back to my bed. I just could not comprehend how I seemed to be excreting so much liquid.

Nevertheless, in all of this discomfort, I could not take my mind off the large crowd of African villagers in the hospital grounds that I had passed on my way in. They were mainly women with babies or small children, many of whom were crying, sitting on the ground in fierce sunshine, most of them with no access to shade. I had no doubt that many of the children and also some of the adults would have been suffering from malaria, just as I was. For them, there was no special treatment, and only the seriously sick, if they were lucky, would get a hospital bed. I also knew that it was not unknown for infants to die in their mother's arms before they received any treatment at all.

I spent a lot of time that first day wondering why a God of love would think that the mosquito was a good idea and worthy of creation. I was not best pleased that I was ill, but the thought of being ill and having to suffer that illness in the way the local population was obliged to, was more than I could bear to contemplate. Later, I was to realise that some children had a persistent form of malaria and spent a lot of their time in hospital. The thought of having recurrent, frequent attacks of malaria was a nightmare as bad as anything that I could imagine. Surely death is better than a lifetime of chronic illness with such awful symptoms?

Two visitors came to see me at the hospital sometime during the first evening. The first one was a married colleague on the school teaching staff who was also an ordained Anglican minister. We did not quite share the same vision of the Gospel—he seemed to me to be concerned with the spread of Anglicanism whereas I was more of a free spirit. I think he was of the opinion that I was a brash young man, full of misplaced enthusiasm and in need of some wise advice. The only thing that I can remember from his visit is that he asked me what I thought God was trying to teach me through this experience. He was perfectly right in all of his assumptions about me. However, I am not sure it was the best time to bring the matter up.

The second visit was from a German Pentecostal missionary. He lived with his family in the town and they led a rather isolated existence as the rest of the expatriate community was English, with the exception of two American missionary families. They did not belong to the local social club as all the other expatriates did, and it was only through a chance meeting with his wife in the town's one grocery store that I ever got to know them. Fortunately, they were both fluent in English and so we became quite friendly.

They were probably as glad of my company as I was of theirs. Working in isolation among African villagers, trying to win converts and establish churches, was a lonely task even for the most dedicated missionaries and it could be particularly lonely for a wife with young children. I was glad of the opportunity to find out as much as I could about the Pentecostal church, this being my first opportunity to become properly acquainted with a person as opposed to having fleeting contact with a pastor.

News travelled very quickly in the local community, though I was surprised when he arrived to visit me and curious to observe that he was bearing bottles of Coca Cola. It was before the days of canned drinks. He said that I needed to drink and that Coca Cola was amazingly good at settling an upset tummy. He knew that if I had malaria, I was certain to have problems of that nature. He opened a bottle and helped me to take some sips. He told me some funny stories about his own experiences with an upset tummy but said that it would pass in a day or two. He eventually left after a brief prayer for my recovery. His visit lifted my spirits considerably, even if I still felt pretty rotten. And he seemed to be right about the Coca Cola!

Early during my second tour of Uganda, I became familiar with the idea, extracted from a literal reading of the Bible, that "*God wants you to be well.*" In these circles, illness was taken to indicate a lack of faith. As I had two further encounters with malaria during my remaining time in Uganda, both unpleasant although not as bad as the first attack, I had to acknowledge that my faith and my experience did not quite tally.

During this second tour I learned something of the fear of living in a society run by a paranoid and ruthless dictator, Idi Amin. Road checks became common. Murders at some of these road checks were reported and there is little doubt that such murders occurred during the process of tribal cleansing. It was said that questions were asked in a particular tribal language and those who did not understand and who were therefore considered to be from the "wrong" tribe were executed. People from the tribe of the ex-president, Milton Obote, were the principal, though not the only, victims of these purges. One favoured method of execution, it is claimed, was to hammer a nail through the temple of a prone victim. Mercifully, I never had to witness such an event though I was well aware that people "went missing".

One raid on our school, during the night, resulted in two local members of staff being questioned and beaten up in front of their families before being taken away. Both reappeared about three weeks later, having suffered considerable mistreatment but at least alive. Friends at other schools informed me that some members of staff had been taken away, never to be seen again.

One particular case sticks in my mind. It concerned a young man at the school where my best friend was teaching, about seventy miles away. He had been married for just five weeks when he was taken from his house at night. It is impossible to imagine the effect of such a traumatic occurrence on his new bride. Without her teacher husband, who never returned, she had no entitlement to a school house. And who knows if she was pregnant?

Thus, I was always apprehensive when I had to stop at a road check. If I was lucky, there would already be a queue of stationary traffic and so I would be aware of the need to stop in good time. However, on two occasions, I inadvertently drove through such checks. Both of these occasions occurred when the only vehicle stopped on the road was a bus. Even though lots of people had disembarked from the bus, I did not realise what was happening. There was no warning sign and no visible sign of any soldiers as I approached. I did not realise that it was a check point until I was in the process of overtaking the bus, travelling at about sixty miles an hour.

I was made aware of my error only when a soldier suddenly appeared beyond the front of the bus waving a rifle. Inevitably, I could not stop in time and came to rest some distance beyond him. I reversed and tried to look contrite, but my travelling companion and I were ordered out of the car and placed before a firing squad before being questioned. The four soldiers had rifles with the magazines attached, almost certainly loaded and ready for firing. They were pointing their rifles straight at us.

Fortunately, my companion had been in East Africa for many years and spoke fluent Swahili. None of the soldiers appeared to speak any English. Equally fortunately, my companion was carrying some government papers which perhaps looked important whether they were or not. He was able to demand to speak with the officer in charge and, after a discussion conducted in Swahili and an examination of our passports, with the officer demanding to see the "diagram", we were allowed to carry on with our journey. The "diagram", the only word in the conversation that I recognised, turned out to be the passport photograph. My companion was of the opinion that the "officer" could not read and hence was uncertain about the importance of the papers that he was carrying. With hindsight, it is probably fortunate that we were carrying our passports. Maybe by that time, carrying passports was normal, even for internal journeys of any distance. My memory is vague on a lot of these details.

During this whole episode, I did not experience any fear. One reason for this is that I did not seriously think that they would dare to shoot British citizens. This assumption was called into question when a white American Peace Corps volunteer was shot dead at such a road check not too long afterwards. I believe that he had been in the country for only three days. The American response was to remove all their government-sponsored workers from Uganda within twenty-four hours. All American citizens were, in fact, advised to leave and given assistance to do so, although one of the two missionary families chose to remain for a short time before relocating to Kenya.

Two of the Peace Corps volunteers who were withdrawn were physics teachers, my colleagues at school. Their departure left me as the only qualified physics teacher in a school of nearly nine hundred students. This experience was to give rise to a number of questions over received wisdom regarding good practice in the teaching profession. I had to develop new teaching strategies, ones that restricted marking to tests only, as there was simply no time for marking routine work. I lectured to entire year groups in the school hall. Solutions to the many problems that I set were pinned up on an enclosed notice board after a short period of time. The examination results suffered a little as a result of all this, though not anything like to the extent that one might have imagined in such unfavourable circumstances. It led me to conclude that a lot of marking, at least in my own subject of physics, was of questionable value and that the time involved could be more profitably spent on preparing better materials for teaching.

On the second occasion that I passed a road check, I was travelling alone. The scenario was almost identical, and I had been overtaking a stationary bus before realising my mistake. Stationary buses were not uncommon on the roads as there were no official bus stops. Buses stopped wherever people wished to get on or off. This would sometimes involve removing personal belongings from the roof rack and would give the impression of a lot of activity. Unloading all belongings from the roof rack was standard procedure at all road checks and there is no doubt that soldiers helped themselves to whatever took their fancy on these occasions.

This time I was confronted by only one soldier and he spoke English. He told me that the penalty for going through an official check was death and he would have to shoot me. I suspected that he was trying to extract a bribe, and I replied that, if he shot me, I would go straight to heaven to be with Jesus, adding that when it came his turn to die, he might not be so lucky for having shot me. This clearly caused some doubt in his mind and he eventually told me to carry on with my journey and be more careful in future. I believed exactly what I said to him and even felt some excitement at the whole idea. I was single at the time and the thought of what effect my death might have had on my mother and two brothers did not cross my mind.

Both of these incidents were to cross my mind, however, on a number of occasions much later on, whenever I began to struggle with increasing uncertainty about my beliefs and the reliability of the Bible. If I had been shot on either of these occasions, then would I not have gone straight to heaven? My faith was probably as great at that time as it was ever destined to be. I harboured no doubts. Subsequently, I could not help wondering why I had been allowed to live and be tormented by considerable doubt. The answer to that question would not come for many years, and when it did, it was certainly not the expected answer or the one I would have wished for.

When I left Uganda after seven (mostly) wonderful years, Idi Amin was still in charge of a nation that seemed to be on the verge of collapse, and all the efforts of a considerable number of expatriate teachers to take the country forward appeared to have been in vain. However, some time ago (August 2009), I met a young woman from Uganda who was in England, working as a missionary. How times change! She was helping out at a local Anglican Church, not the Church that I attended but very close to where I live. She told me that Uganda had many universities (as opposed to one when I was there) and that some parts of Uganda were thriving, though not, regrettably, the area where I had been teaching.

If she was anything to go by, education in Uganda had certainly not ground to a halt. It was tremendously gratifying to know that progress can sometimes be maintained even in the most unpromising of situations. The medical department at the university that I attended is now working in co-operation with a medical school in one of the outlying towns in Uganda that consisted only of a few shops, a secondary school, and possibly a small hospital when I was there. It was further gratifying proof that all had not been in vain.

Unfortunately, Uganda has also been in the news over the past two years for quite other reasons, namely its proposals for fiercely homophobic legislation, supported by senior Anglican clergy, including the Archbishop, Henry Orombi. I knew Henry when he was a student at a theological college on the outskirts of the capital, Kampala, and I had more contact with him when he came to England for further study. He was another extremely gifted, charming, charismatic young man and I was convinced that he would have a great future. What I never imagined is that he would become an arch-conservative, fundamentalist homophobe. Once we were united by a common experience of salvation and a common passion to serve our God. Sadly, there no longer exists any bond to remind us of the young people we once were.

Shortly after writing all this, I came across news that David Kato, who was considered a founding father of the gay rights movement in Uganda, was found bludgeoned to death in his home in Kampala on 26 January 2011. Although the extremely homophobic police force say that the motive may have been one of theft, it is difficult not to concur with the statement issued by Val Kalende, the chairwoman of one of Uganda's gay rights groups. She says: "*David's death is the result of the hatred planted in Uganda by US evangelicals in 2009.*" James Nsaba Buturo, Uganda's minister of ethics and integrity, who describes himself as a devout Christian, has said "*Homosexuals can forget about human rights.*"

Uganda is one of the most devoutly Christian countries on the planet and it is also one of the most homophobic. The proposed law to execute people for certain homosexual acts is still pending on the statute books. Only the strong disapproval of many countries who give aid to Uganda has, at the time of writing, prevented it from becoming law.

One interesting incident occurred shortly before I finally left Uganda. I was "arrested" by police at my house and taken to the police station in the local town. There I was spoken to by the senior police officer for the district, who used an official and rather serious tone of voice. He informed me that he had become concerned about some of my activities. In particular, he warned me against saying anything that could be construed as being critical of the government. After several minutes of this he suddenly announced that he had said what he was obliged to say to me and that he was now going to speak "*off the record.*"

He wanted to know if it was true that I was intending to leave Uganda in the near future. When I confirmed this, he spent ten minutes or so trying to convince me to change my mind, because, he said, Uganda had been deserted by almost everybody in its time of need and they desperately wanted people such as myself to stay on and help with the education of the students.

I was, by this time, the only expatriate teacher left on the school staff, although there was an old Catholic missionary still attached to the school who spent most of his time trying to undo the Reformation.

At some point in this conversation, the fact that I was also intending to visit Kenya one last time must have come up. He then wrote a short letter and put it into an envelope, together with a hundred-shilling note, quite a lot of money in those days. The envelope was addressed to his son who was apparently at school in Kenya. He gave me the name of some official to ask for at the Uganda side of the border control who would facilitate my passage across the border. I was to deliver the letter to another official (who was apparently a relative) on the Kenya side of the border, if at all possible. He did not trust the postal system, he said, but he trusted me to deliver the envelope because I was "*one of the saved ones.*" I duly delivered his letter when I made the trip soon afterwards.

Chapter 4   PERU AND MARRIAGE

As the situation in Uganda deteriorated, my economic situation deteriorated with it, until survival without outside help became just about impossible. As I did not have this outside help towards the end, when the British government cancelled all further teaching contracts, I was obliged to call it a day. I left with a heavy heart but had the good fortune to acquire another teaching job soon after arriving back in England. This time it was to be in a private British school in Lima, Peru. The students that I was to teach were almost entirely affluent Peruvians but it was to prove great fun and provide further opportunities to observe and to participate in Christian activity. I was to spend the next six years in this beautiful country.

Although the Roman Catholic Church had a dominant, all-pervasive influence in Peru, the Pentecostal Church, which was already very strong in Puerto Rico, had started to extend its influence further south and Peru was beginning to feel that influence. Once I had learned enough Spanish, I was able to involve myself with an Anglican charismatic group and also with one of the local Pentecostal churches, and thus gain further experience and insight into how the Gospel was able to thrive in quite different cultures. I also encountered a wonderful group of missionaries called the Wycliffe Bible Translators.

These missionaries first learned Spanish, the national language of Peru, although it was by no means the language of all Peruvians. Then, because their work was focussed on the non-Spanish speaking, indigenous population, they moved out into tribal areas, usually in the Amazon jungle (now more commonly referred to as a rainforest), and proceeded to learn a tribal language from scratch. There were no books to consult as nobody had ever committed these languages to writing.

I could only marvel at the techniques that had been developed by a number of gifted linguists within the society for learning a tribal language just by living amongst the people. The main purpose of this was to translate the Bible into the native language and make its message available. This, in turn, required the people, more especially the younger ones, to be able to read and write. So the establishment of basic schooling became a part of the work. Training in such matters as agriculture and hygiene had always been emphasised with the intention of trying to improve general health and to reduce the incidence of debilitating illnesses. Spanish was also taught in an effort to help the tribal people integrate more effectively into mainstream Peruvian society and also to provide the opportunity for young students to join the state education system.

Over time it has become possible for such people to progress all the way to degree level in one of the national universities. Such a mighty oak has blossomed from such a tiny acorn, the idea of one man, Cameron Townsend, way back in the 1920s. One great privilege for me was to meet a girl from one of the tribes of the Amazon Rainforest who had just qualified as a doctor in one of the medical schools in Lima. She was returning to her tribe to be their doctor and to help in educating the next generation as well as to help build up a local church.

In addition to meeting a number of the missionaries, I was also privileged to meet the founder of the society, Cameron Townsend, the man whose remarkable vision and life story I had already read about. At the same event I also met a man whose life had been drastically altered by his encounter with one of the missionaries in Cameron Townsend's organisation of Bible translators. He was known as Chief Tariri and he had been the head of the Shipibo tribe, a sub-group of the Candoshi Indians in the Amazon Rainforest.

In stature, he was not impressive, barely reaching my shoulders in height, although it has to be admitted that he was quite old at the time, certainly well past his prime. His reputation, however, was something else. He had arrived at his position of chief in a time honoured way—by removing all those who stood between him and the throne. Through a translator, I was told by this grateful man of the many benefits that had come to his tribe as a result of the work of the missionaries. "*Once we died in groups,*" he said, referring to the incidence of plague, "*now we die one at a time.*"

The incredible story of Chief Tariri has been told in a book called *Tariri: My Story—From Jungle Killer to Christian Missionary*, first published in 1965. Two particular questions he asked me remain indelibly etched within my mind to this day. The first was to ask how long my people had known this good news about Jesus Christ. I replied that it was well over a thousand years. His second question was to ask why it had taken us so long to bring this message to his people.

As a post-script, he himself might have been a greater beneficiary than most from the arrival of Christianity. It might have prevented him from losing his throne and possibly his life to some young usurper as he himself had once been. As it was, he seemed to have been allowed to fade away gracefully. At the time I met him, his influence on the tribe was no longer what it once had been, or so I was told.

My time in Peru certainly had its wonderful moments on the spiritual front, but it also had experiences of a less beneficial kind. I had a recurrent problem with a fever, not frequent, but when it surfaced it could last for several days. Such fevers occurred only at nights, and would nearly always subside by morning. I was convinced that I was suffering from some form of residual malaria similar to that which plagued many African children, though I was not sure. Uncertainty in matters of illness can be very frightening. If you do not know what is wrong with you, you cannot be certain that there is a cure.

Once again, I was troubled by the considerable number of people who lived in the poorer quarters. I had access to the best medical help available whereas they often had little or no access to any help. I knew that tuberculosis was still a problem among these people, and I wondered what it would be like to suffer from recurrent fevers, with little medical relief, no guarantee of a cure and the real possibility that you would die from your illness.

I also knew that people the world over, in previous generations, had suffered particularly unpleasant and often slow deaths from all kinds of illnesses. Even today, I sometimes look at eighteenth and nineteenth century gravestones in English churchyards and notice how many of the victims were children, evidence of the grim realities of life in those times. What none of this provides evidence for is the existence of a loving and powerful God, and that is what worried me.

Working in Peru meant that I had plenty of opportunities to travel around. I visited the wondrous site of Machu Picchu and ancient temples in the mountainous interior. On one wonderful trip I travelled down the Ucayali River, a tributary of the Amazon River, which winds its way through the rainforest. The experience of travelling on an old river boat (I think that it was steam-driven and used wood as a fuel) was akin to being transported into another age. The trip down river lasted a whole day. In the evening, thousands of hungry mosquitoes suddenly descended upon the boat. We had not been forewarned of this eventuality and my only protection from them was a poncho that I carried with me.

The boat pulled into the bank shortly afterwards and we spent the night ashore, sleeping in a typical Indian dwelling, part and parcel of the trip. It was not a pleasant experience as the entire evening and much of the night were spent in a desperate attempt to keep the mosquitoes at bay. Trying to cover myself in a poncho in such humid heat was exceedingly uncomfortable, although not nearly as bad as being bitten. The Indians fared no better, and all used thick blankets to protect themselves. Blankets offered more protection than a typical poncho.

The Amazon Rainforest may seem an exotic place in photographs, but after sunset, it is as close to a hell on earth as I can possibly imagine. I could not understand why anybody would ever want to live there, until the next day, when the sun came up, the mosquitoes had disappeared and the rainforest was transformed into something quite beautiful. We stayed for the day and another night, meeting the local school children and sampling native food among other things, before making the return trip back up the river on the third day. Travelling against the flow of the water meant slower progress, though I no longer remember if we had to spend a night on the boat. The children that we had encountered during our stay were delightful and fortunately spoke some Spanish as this was obviously a tourist spot.

The owner of the boat, who was also its Captain, was Jewish and he was assisted by his grown-up daughter. They were both more than happy to chat to the passengers in Spanish. Both of them had been on the point of going to live in Israel in 1967 when the Six-Day War between Israel and a coalition of Arab States (Egypt, Syria and Jordan) erupted. They never made the trip and now spent their lives ferrying people up and down the Ucayali River. They were just two of the many fascinating people that I was privileged to meet on my travels.

There was another encounter that stuck in my mind for a very different reason. I was visiting the city of Huaraz in the Peruvian highlands from where there are stunning views of Huascarán, the highest peak in the Cordillera Blanca. On Sunday morning I took time off from travelling and sightseeing to visit a local Pentecostal church. The preacher was a visitor and he told the congregation of the marvellous move of God that was occurring in his own church in the capital,

Lima; of answered prayers, healings and great church growth. He then began to exhort the congregation to have faith and believe for the same sort of things in their own church.

When I spoke to him after the service and told him that I also lived in Lima and would love to visit his church, he became strangely evasive, claiming that the church was very difficult to find. I think that what he meant was that the church that he had been describing would be impossible to find because it almost certainly did not exist outside of his imagination.

Exaggeration was not the only problem that seemed to afflict the churches. The Anglican Church in Lima, which had been founded to service the large British contingent that had once worked in the cotton trade, was still attended by many expatriates and even some missionaries from the USA, as well as some of the more educated Peruvians. On one occasion, this church was privileged to have a very distinguished visiting preacher from Britain, Alan Redpath. During his sermon, he told some anecdote about a pastor of a church, someone he claimed to know and who worked in Britain close to where Alan himself was working at the time that this occurred. This pastor apparently had the habit of going to a railway bridge and throwing his hat into the air every time a train passed. Questioned about this strange behaviour, he replied that a train was one the few things in the area that could move without his having to push it.

Oddly, I had recently read a book which contained exactly the same anecdote, except that it was set somewhere in America. Mr Redpath seemed to be very uncomfortable when I mentioned this to him at the end of the service but he insisted that it had indeed happened as he described. Apart from the fact that it is a very unlikely story, even if it does make a point, the fact that such stories, true or invented, could be retold and set in different places, reminded me strongly of some Bible stories that appear to be set in different locations in different Gospels. Perhaps the same process that was evident at end of the twentieth century was also at work nearly two thousand years earlier when the Gospels were being written down.

There is one benefit from the time that I spent in in Peru that I must mention. It was here that I met the girl who was later to become my wife. We met in Trujillo, a coastal city over three hundred miles (about 500 km) north of Lima. I had gone there to spend the long summer holidays with the family of a friend in order to try and learn to speak Spanish. My future wife was at the local university and English formed part of her degree course. We thus had an immediate common interest: we were trying to learn each other's language. It certainly provided me with a massive incentive to learn Spanish!

After we were married, our first two children were born in Peru. For various reasons we then came to England where I was to spend the next twenty-eight years teaching physics. I began in a comprehensive school, but found this very difficult after teaching in Africa and Peru. Fortunately I managed to transfer to a large, private school not too long afterwards. England provided me with my first experience of teaching girls.

My wife and I soon became members of one of the independent charismatic churches that were becoming more and more common at the time. My experience with this church was also very positive. It was a large, friendly, confident church and again had an extremely committed membership and seemed to have excellent leadership. So I was very happy, although by now I had read the entire Bible and the seeds of doubt regarding claims made for its inerrancy had begun to grow in my mind. It was only much later, after my son had come out to us, that I discovered a much darker, and to me unacceptable, side of evangelical Christianity.

Chapter 5   THE BIRTH OF OUR SON

The onset of my wife's third pregnancy occurred when we had come to England and was accompanied by very severe sickness. This caused her to spend her first Christmas in England in the local hospital. The hospital staff, however, appeared to think that the severity of the sickness was caused by the fact that she was unhappy about her pregnancy and was subconsciously rejecting it.

The reality was that my wife had always dreamed of having a large family, close together in age, and so the gynaecologist's diagnosis did little for her state of mind. She was desperately unhappy and was also experiencing considerable homesickness as this was her first Christmas away from her family in Peru.

However, when a scan, done shortly after Christmas Day, revealed that she was expecting twins, the attitude of the hospital staff suddenly changed. My wife was ecstatic and her condition began to improve so that soon she wanted to be out of the hospital and at home. As I was on school holiday and would be able to look after her, at least for a while, she took the risk of discharging herself. Fortunately, her health continued to improve, and although she still felt sick, she was able to keep down enough food and drink to stay alive.

Eventually, the sickness disappeared altogether and we were able to settle down to await the new additions to our family. My wife is one who likes to prepare well in advance and she spent time choosing all the things she thought we would need when the twins came along. We even had the pleasure of having one of my wife's younger sisters from Peru come to visit us. Somehow we had managed to get a six month visa for her and fortunately she had arrived well before the birth was expected. Our happiness knew no limits.

One hot evening, in the middle of June, my wife startled me by saying that she thought she had had a contraction. This was surprising because the birth was not expected until early August. We drove to the hospital as a precaution where they confirmed that she was indeed going into labour. The decision was taken to transport her to a nearby, much larger hospital that had incubators available. Clearly it was felt that the birth of twins, several weeks prematurely, was a cause for some concern.

I remember being in a waiting room anxiously trying to pass the time but at least grateful that my sister-in-law was at our house looking after our other two children. Eventually, at around ten o'clock, the surgeon came out and said that the twins were two boys and that they were both doing well. Unfortunately, my wife was sedated after a Caesarean section (our previous children had also been born that way) and I would not be able to see the babies before morning, so he recommended that I go home, get some sleep and come back the next day.

My sleep that night was interrupted by a loud knocking on the door. I arose and immediately felt panic. People rarely knock on your door with such urgency at two o'clock in the morning bearing good news. It was, in fact, a policewoman, and she told me that the hospital wanted me to go back immediately. She did not know why, but I could guess. I knew instinctively that one or possibly both twins were either dead or in serious danger of immediate death. In the event one had died, and the second twin was in intensive care, with, I was informed, less than a fifty-fifty chance of surviving. Both twins had suffered from respiratory distress syndrome. Did I want them to call a priest?

I replied instantly that I did not want any priest and that the child would live and I passionately believed that he would. I felt desolate and devastated that they had not told me of any problems until it was too late for one of our babies. If I had been able to pray, surely both of them could have been saved? Despite the dreadful shock, I was confident that now I was able to pray, at least the second child would pull through. The possibility that we might lose both of the twins simply did not bear thinking about. I drove away from the hospital but did not head for home. Instead I drove to the house of our Bible study group leader to tell him the news. I can rarely remember praying so fervently.

On reaching the house, sometime after 3 a.m., I was invited in and given some coffee to drink. While his wife tried to be consoling and prayed for the life of our remaining twin, the husband was on the phone, contacting other senior members of the church. Although I did not know it at the time, this triggered a chain reaction and soon, not only were large numbers of people from our own church interceding for our child, but also members from several related churches around the country were involved. My own confidence remained high. I could not believe that God would allow Satan to snatch both of our twins from us.

Nevertheless, my confidence was not quite so high once we had been allowed to see our child. My wife was taken to the special care baby unit in a wheelchair. Both of us had to don gowns and wash our hands before we were allowed to enter the intensive care room. Here there were several incubators and our tiny baby was in one of them, tubes and needles entering or leaving his body at several different places. He wore only a small nappy and his skin was a sallow yellow colour. We were told that he was jaundiced and that was the reason for the ultra-violet lamp which also meant that his eyes had to be bandaged. He was hooked up to a breathing machine and supplied with oxygen-enriched air. I discovered that that it was much easier to have faith when the problem was not so immediately visible.

We were each allowed to put a hand into the incubator and touch him, and I prayed as I did so, with rather less bravado than I had had before and grateful for the prayer support of so many others. There is undoubted strength to be drawn from numbers. I could tell that my wife was very distressed and was desperate to hold him, fearing that, as had happened with her other twin, she might be denied the chance of ever holding him when he was alive. I think that we were allowed two visits each day and this draining situation lasted for about a week as our precious baby tenaciously clung to life.

Thankfully, he slowly began to improve and was eventually able to breathe for himself, although he still needed an oxygen enriched atmosphere and his head was placed inside a plastic dome. Then the day arrived when he could be taken out of the incubator for a few minutes and at last my wife was allowed to hold him.

It was a huge uplift for her. Although he remained in intensive care for over two weeks, he finally won his fight for life and we were eventually allowed to take him home. Before that day came, however, there was another traumatic duty to perform.

My wife had not been allowed to see her dead baby in the hospital. She had longed to see and hold his body, to say goodbye, but he had already been placed in the morgue by the time she awoke the morning after the birth. She was allowed out of the hospital on the day of the funeral and I collected our dead child to take him home and put him into the little coffin that I had made for him. He was frozen completely solid, deep scars being visible where the coroner had made incisions. My wife was consumed with grief and her tears flowed freely. Somehow, I managed to control my own grief until after the burial, but at that point I too broke down. Only then did the finality of the tragedy come home to me. The dreams that we had had for the last six months were now, at least partly, in ruins.

Fortunately, the school summer holidays were coming and in any case, I think that I had been given indefinite, compassionate leave. This was before fathers were entitled to paternity leave. My wife and I could therefore look forward to spending several weeks together as we struggled to come to terms with all that had happened. Also, there was a good chance that our surviving twin would soon be coming come home to join us. It did not remove our sense of loss, but no doubt it helped us to cope better than we otherwise might have done. This child was also our miracle child – the child who survived by the grace of God and the prayers of God's people.

A few days after he had been allowed to join us, I was stricken with an acute appendicitis and was hospitalised myself for a week. I was very conscious that without medical intervention, neither I nor my son would have been alive. While I was grateful that both of us were alive, I could not help wondering how these recent events could be squared with my fundamental belief in the idea that "*God wants you to be well.*" Wasn't sickness something that only the heathen should suffer from?

Chapter 6   GROWING UP

Being a premature twin, our son was quite small at birth, weighing in at just two and a half kilos. He was to remain on the small side for most of his growing years, almost as if he was a year younger than his birth certificate said he was. He was not very sporting, which may have been a blessing given that premature babies seem to be at greater risk of brain injury. He did, however, learn to swim and he later took an interest in tennis, although, like me, his interest never translated into anything beyond basic competence. On the other hand, he seemed to be quite bright and he was a quick learner.

It was my wife who was the first to detect what she thought was the occasional effeminate mannerism or trait in him, though to my less discerning eye, he had always seemed be a normal boy. He never played with his sister's dolls, but was fascinated with Thomas the Tank Engine from an early age and would ask for Thomas electric train sets every Christmas. By the time he was six he was the proud owner of Henry the green engine, Thomas the tank engine and Gordon the blue engine. We had a lot of track and I was rather thrilled to have a son who shared one of my own passions. His elder brother had shown no interest at all in train sets. He preferred Action Man and other toys that did not appeal to me.

As a boy, I also had had a series of Hornby train sets for Christmas. Mine were clockwork. I never received the much longed-for electric train set because my father feared all things electrical and was sure that I would electrocute myself. Perhaps, however, electric train sets were just too expensive; I will never know. The bodywork of these clockwork train sets that I received was made of tin as far as I can remember, and they must have been rather flimsy because they never lasted from one Christmas to the next, which is why I had the same Christmas present three or four years running.

Eventually they became stronger, or I became more careful, because I did manage to keep the last two sets and still had them, together with many accessories, when I left for university. On one occasion when I returned for vacation, they had disappeared. My mother had given them away to some neighbour's boy because, she said, he had no toys to play with. The truth is they occupied a lot of space and my mother was glad to be rid of them. I had waited a long time to get any sort of replacement.

As our son grew older, he graduated to playing with Meccano sets, building complex models with the use of metal frames, nuts, bolts, wheels and pulleys, spanners and screwdrivers and other devices that mimicked the real world of engineering. There can be few toys that are so obviously made for boys. Later still, when the computer age was really beginning to take off, he acquired a passion for violent video games, Street Fighter II being the one that I remember, and both he and his elder brother played this game together.

My daughter never showed any interest in such games. Consequently, the alarm bells which occasionally sounded in my wife's head had never sounded in mine; or maybe the real truth is that it is difficult to bring yourself to acknowledge unpalatable truths and this can easily cause you to be very selective when dealing with evidence that you would rather did not exist.

One thing that was obvious was that our son had a very caring nature and he always wanted some sort of pet to look after. I remember the day that he arrived home with a goldfish in a water-filled polythene bag that he had won at some local fair. We had that goldfish for the next few years. He then wanted budgerigars and we kept three or four in a small aviary in the garden.

My wife was also fond of animals but our son suffered from asthma and we were unable to keep house pets at that time. She had to be content with keeping guinea pigs in the garden for a while and when they died she took to keeping rabbits. He was noticeably more affectionate towards these animals than his elder brother was. Only when he was seventeen years old and his asthma seemed to have become less of a problem did we acquire a small and not very hairy dog, a replacement for the older two children who had both left home at the same time to go to university.

The first inklings that I had were certainly slow in coming. By the age of fourteen, our eldest child was already displaying an active interest in girls and had his first girlfriend. The following year, we had a family holiday in Spain and this time our eldest was plainly bored with family activities and wanted to go by himself to the swimming pool. We discovered that there was a blonde girl at this swimming pool who had caught his eye. On the same holiday, my daughter also became interested in a boy in the teenage disco that the eldest two attended in the evenings.

My wife and I watched this development with some amusement, although we were really caught off balance. With our daughter, particularly, it all seemed to happen so quickly. Neither of us had ever talked to our children to explain that they had now reached the point where they should be taking an interest in the opposite sex. It all occurred as a matter of course and was the first sign that the inner drives that mark the transition from child to adult were already present. Adolescence had arrived. It was a natural phenomenon, outside the control of any one of us and all we could really do was to accept it, while trying to lay down some ground rules to keep things within safe bounds.

Having observed the way our first two children responded to the onset of puberty, we should have been a little surprised when our son did not follow the same pattern. However, he had always been different in that he did not make friends as easily. Perhaps, deep down, there was always this fundamental difference in him, the reason for which would not become apparent until much later.

We were aware that school was not a happy time for him particularly when he was in the sixth form. His academic progress, which had led to an outstanding set of GCSE results, began to slip, although he did well enough to get to a good university to study Computer Science. Here his academic focus returned, to such an extent that he managed to obtain a degree with First Class Honours. Although this delighted us, we were concerned about the social scene. There had been no sign of any girlfriend and no obvious sign of many friends at all.

We had hoped that university would provide a different environment for him, one where he would meet more people with similar interests, and we grew more anxious when this did not seem to be the case, although perhaps we reached false conclusions from his obvious reluctance to talk at all about his private life. Indeed, almost since his birth, we had worried about him far more than we ever did about the other two. Perhaps the circumstances of his birth made a difference. Maybe we need to face the possibility of losing something before we can appreciate its true value.

Such had been our relief and gratitude when he pulled through as a new-born baby that he had a very special place in our hearts. Love makes you worry. And we worried that somehow, we did not seem able to understand, or connect with our youngest son as we had been able to do with the other two. Our son always seemed to be a little different in a way that we could never quite define.

Chapter 7   THE QUEST FOR HEALING

After his graduation, our youngest son got a job close to the university where he had studied and he continued to live away from home. His excellent degree had boosted his confidence and so we hoped that he would find the world of work more to his liking and that he would find making friends a little easier. Of course, deep down, this meant we hoped that he might meet a girl. Universities are very large places and it is sometimes easy to be lost in a crowd. Our hopes in this area lasted for a further six months, up to that fateful Boxing Day.

Like any committed Christian confronted with a problem that ran contrary to one's beliefs, I began to prepare in earnest for a major spiritual battle. This included regular fasting, increased amounts of time spent in Bible study and prayer, and increased levels of giving in the belief that if I looked after God's interests, he would take care of mine. Bible study became more specific as I focussed on promises relating to the children of believers. I confessed these promises aloud to bolster my faith. I put my faith into action in all sorts of little ways, such as buying presents for the grandchildren that one day I hope to have, always buying three of each present so that the future children of my youngest son were always included. I held the vision of my son walking down the church aisle, towards some beautiful young girl, constantly before me. No stone was to be left unturned in my efforts to see my son "delivered". My God was a big God, and if he condemned homosexuality, then surely he would provide healing.

Saturday was the day that I chose for fasting as this seemed least likely to cause conflict with my teaching commitments. It turned out not to be the best choice because Saturday was the day of the week that my wife found most difficult to cope with. There had once been a time when the entire day would have been focussed on the children's needs, but these times were now gone. It didn't happen suddenly, which is possibly why I had not realised the full extent of the vacuum that had been left behind. Children gradually become adults and become independent of their parents. For someone like my wife, whose greatest fulfilment in life came from being a mother, this slow change left her like a boat that had slowly come adrift from its mooring. The focus, and indeed the raison d'être of her life, had disappeared.

For a number of years, my wife had had some part-time work, giving craft classes that had been arranged for Asian women suffering from depression. This gave some structure to the weekdays and even Sundays had some sort of routine, based around the church. But there was an emptiness to her Saturdays that was to become more acute now that we would not even be sharing meals together. My decision meant that whatever cracks there might have been in our marriage were about to become very much wider.

This state of affairs lasted a year until the following Boxing Day when my son announced that he had some good news for us—he had a boyfriend. The shock of this was comparable to his announcement the previous year. I was devastated as it seemed that all my efforts had been ignored by God. Neither my wife nor I were able to show any feeling of joy and this was clearly apparent to our son. It was obvious that we were treating him differently. We had no problem sharing in the happiness of our other children when they told us of their girlfriends and boyfriends, as he angrily pointed out to us, but we did not appear to be interested in his happiness.

He had a point. But there was also something else. Before he told us of this development, I had noticed that he had seemed happier, more relaxed, more open and easier to talk to this Christmas than he had been on previous occasions. Sadly, we had suddenly put a damper on this apparent improvement, although I did ask if he would be happy for me to meet this boyfriend in the near future.

The unfortunate reality was that my faith had taken another severe knock. To have a homosexually inclined son was one thing. To have a son who was a practising homosexual was quite another. Had my son passed the point of no return? Feelings of panic began to surface. No immediate meeting with his boyfriend was arranged and I continued my quest for my son's deliverance, although I continued to try and keep this a secret from him.

I was in the habit of watching the Christian broadcasts on satellite television at every opportunity to learn everything that I could about receiving God's promises. There were a lot of homophobic speakers who appeared on these programmes, however, and my wife came to resent them. I was eventually obliged to stop watching them whenever she was around, since my doing so was causing increasing tension between us.

Nevertheless, one evening, my wife went out to the local supermarket and I availed myself of the opportunity to switch on a broadcast once again. I can remember very vividly that the programme featured a speaker by the name of (Dr) Tony Campolo. He was from America and was the invited speaker at an evangelical Christian conference which was at the British seaside resort of Eastbourne. I had heard of Dr. Campolo and knew that he had made quite a reputation for himself, but I had never actually heard him speak. He was now about to say something that would shake me to the core. His talk broached the subject of homosexuality in the world today and he said that "*nobody has the faintest idea what causes homosexuality and nobody has the slightest idea how to cure it, **despite the extravagant claims (of healing) made by many evangelical Christian organisations**.*"

Here was a respected insider (at the time), admitting to what nobody else in the evangelical world dared to say. I had just been told that homosexuality was not what I had always been led to believe that it was − namely a perversion that could be cured with the right treatment or attitude. It became clear in that moment that I needed to do some serious research to try and find out what I was actually up against and to discover what, if anything, was reliably known about this condition. If I understood the problem properly, then perhaps I would be in a better position to confront it.

I began to search the Internet for anything relevant and the first site that made any impression on me was one called *Courage UK,* which turned out to be a gay-affirming organisation founded by Jeremy Marks, a gay evangelical Christian (if that is not a contradiction in terms). Jeremy turned out to have a fascinating story that was also to have a profound effect on my own views. He knew that he was gay from an early age but still became a committed, Bible-believing Christian at the age of 21. Although he continued to struggle with his own sexuality, he entered full-time ministry under the auspices of the House Church movement and had special involvement with gay Christians.

In 1987 he undertook training in California with an organisation called *Love in Action* which ran a "*Steps out of Homosexuality*" programme. Back in England, in 1988, he set up *Courage UK*, dedicated to helping people (including himself!) to step out of homosexuality. In 1991 he entered into a heterosexual marriage, although I believe that his wife, also an evangelical Christian, was fully aware of his homosexuality. In the mid-1990s his reputation was such that he was offered, and accepted, an invitation to become the President of Exodus International Europe, the European arm of the American organisation that, since its inception in 1976, has promoted "*Freedom from homosexuality through the power of Jesus Christ.*"

Essentially, if anybody could lay claims to be an expert in the field of homosexuality, then surely it was Jeremy Marks. Yet, despite all the conferences, support meetings, prayer meetings, "claiming the promises" meetings, Bible study and fasting, Jeremy admits that over a fourteen year period, neither his own organisation nor Exodus International Europe could point to one single case of a successful change in sexual orientation. He himself remained a gay man even though he was in a heterosexual marriage. He honestly admits that for all their belief and commitment to the programme, they might have done more harm than good. He mentioned incidents of people self-harming out of desperation because they found no change at all in the nature of their sexual drive.

Eventually, accepting the inevitable, he left Exodus and changed the ethos of his own organisation, *Courage UK*, to become a gay-affirming ministry. It did not take long for the evangelicals, who had fully supported his more orthodox, or in their eyes more acceptable, approach to homosexuals to regard him as a renegade and a pariah to be avoided.

The *Courage UK* website contains many testimonies from gay Christians and a list of recommended books to read. Two of the recommended books I found to be hugely revealing. They both tell similar stories. The first book was called *Stranger at the Gate* by Mel White. The second was *A Life of Unlearning* by Anthony Venn-Brown. Mel is an American, Anthony an Australian. Both of these men were married and had children and both had hugely successful Christian ministries. Both were also gay and knew that unless they could find a cure and become heterosexuals, their marriages and their ministries would collapse. Both men had married without admitting their sexual orientation in the hope that being in a heterosexual marriage would bring a cure of its own accord. They were both mistaken.

The books then describe the incredible lengths that each of them went to in order to find "healing". This included attending ex-gay camps run by supposedly ex-gay Christians of the sort overseen by Exodus

International, as well as undergoing such things as fasting over a twenty day period to "seek healing from God." They had counselling from professional Christian psychologists; they were prayed for many times and on several occasions they fully believed that they had been healed. Freedom from the "problem", however, was never more than temporary; the lion could not be killed and keeping it in its cage always proved to be too difficult a task. Inevitably, both of these men were finally overwhelmed; neither was able to carry on coping with the pressures of living a lie. Their marriages collapsed and both were removed from their ministries and were cast out from the communities of the chosen.

I was now confronted by something that put me in a very uncomfortable position. If there were seriously committed, gay Christians, who had been unable to change their sexual orientation, then what chance did my son have? And where, exactly, was God in all this? Worse was to follow. I found the site of an organisation called True Freedom Trust (*TfT*), founded by Martin Hallett, another gay Christian. The purpose of this organisation now focuses on support for homosexual Christian people in their endeavours to live a celibate lifestyle, although I think that originally he entertained the hope that a change in sexual orientation could be effected. Long experience, no doubt coupled with disappointment, appears to have convinced him that such change is at best unlikely, though he seems to shy away from admitting that it may be not be possible.

Martin had written a book, *Still Learning to Love*, in which he describes his own journey in coming to terms both with his sexuality and the faith which came to him at some later date. I read this book and also a lot of the literature put out by *TfT* and I corresponded with Martin very briefly. I sent him a DVD of a *Lifetime Movies* film, *Prayers for Bobby,* the tragic story of a homosexual boy driven to suicide by his inability to come to terms with his homosexual orientation. He had not been helped by pressure from an over-zealous Christian mother. I wrote a letter to Martin to express my concern that his particular take on the issue of homosexuality and Christianity was the sort of thing that appeared to have driven Bobby Griffith (and no doubt others) to commit suicide and was therefore highly questionable. I never received any reply to my specific question in that letter and do not know if he ever watched the film.

After much thought, I decided that I could not agree with the stance taken by TfT. I had witnessed the huge difference that occurred with my son now that he felt able to be openly gay and have the same opportunity for love and relationships as his brother and sister. He became happy, more confident, and much easier (for us) to talk to. These are not insignificant gains to be discarded for the greater good of preserving the morality of the nation or even defending the authority of the Bible. They are of fundamental importance to the wellbeing of any human being. I still do not know why this particular activity between two consenting adults should cause a God who made the universe to become upset. I rather suspect that it has a great deal to do with the endless obsession that the human race seems to have with the issue of sex *per se*, not to mention the prurient interest displayed by some in the sex life of others.

Sex is a basic drive in almost every human being. It is something that is very hard to escape from and is equally difficult to dominate. This is something that clearly has troubled my sex for a very long time, certainly since Bible times. We are obsessed with it but we also seem to fear it to some extent. Men blame women for providing the temptation that many of them cannot resist (recall the story of Adam and Eve) and hence there is a distrust of women.

This distrust may find expression in the attitude of the Roman Catholic Church that makes celibacy a requirement for the priesthood. Abstaining from sex apparently elevates people to a higher spiritual plane. Put another way, indulgence in sexual activity must relegate us to some morally inferior state. It is small wonder that the Roman Catholic Church in France in the 1950s seemed to equate Brigitte Bardot with the devil incarnate for her role in Roger Vadim's film *And God Created Woman*.

There is some biblical sanction for all this. One perfectly reasonable interpretation of the Bible verse found in Leviticus 15:18 might suggest that God himself finds sex distasteful. Having sex always results in a man suffering at least temporary separation from this God who, seemingly, must have created sex solely for the purpose of procreation. It is an idea that persists, and is possibly why homosexual sex just cannot be tolerated and why the Catholic Church officially forbids contraception.

The latter policy is responsible for much misery in developing countries where poorer families are often unable to cope with the number of children that they have and are unable to access any means of birth control. Many children from such families in Latin America end up on the streets or in one of the many

Catholic orphanages to be found there. The need for orphanages would not be removed, but it would almost certainly be reduced, by a more flexible and enlightened approach to contraception from the Catholic Church.

I was aware as I contemplated all these things that my view of the Bible was beginning to change. As my knowledge of homosexuality increased, I realised that this new knowledge seemed to be at odds with what evangelical (and other) Christians believe. Rarely did I read of anyone who claimed that they had chosen to be a homosexual (before being convinced of the error or their ways). I was, instead, reading of a great many who had unsuccessfully fought against their homosexual inclinations. What did it all mean?

Chapter 8   THE TURNING POINT

In May, 1988, Tony Campolo visited the city where I live and I went to listen to him speak. In reality, I was probably more interested in meeting his wife, who I knew had a ministry of her own to homosexual people and took a more positive approach than her husband in that she believed in the value of, and in the right of, gay and lesbian people to form partnerships. Her husband stood by the more traditional view that such people should remain celibate to remain within the will of God.

I introduced myself to her immediately after her husband had finished speaking and I was at once impressed by her concern for my "plight". She turned out to be a very sweet, understanding lady whose experience and knowledge of the homosexual world far exceeded mine. She was to recommend further books which she believed would help me and in this she was certainly right. The first was a book called *Prayers for Bobby,* written by Leroy Adams, himself a gay man, and published in 1995 by Harper Collins. Later it was made into an inspirational film for television by *Lifetime Movies.* The film, now available on DVD, has already been mentioned.

However, one or two further points should be noted. Bobby was given counselling by a professional, Christian psychologist, in addition to "help" from his local church. Both of these were at best ineffective but more probably were detrimental to his well-being, pushing him further towards his eventual suicide in August 1983. Part of the book is based around a secret diary that Bobby kept during the years of his struggle, detailing his frustrations and descent into final, suicidal despair. The diary came to light only after his death. Bobby's mother, Mary, who came to accept her own part in this tragic story, subsequently became a prominent campaigner for the rights of the LGBT community in the USA. She is an inspirational person, though not in the eyes of evangelical Christians. I would strongly advise anyone to visit any of the many websites devoted to Mary Griffith and *Prayers for Bobby*. One particularly good site can be found by typing *Gay Teenage Suicide-Gay Youth Suicide-Bobby Griffith-Mary Griffith* into Google or any other search engine.

It was a traumatic reading experience for me because Mary Griffith's beliefs and aims were identical to mine. We had clearly approached the problem differently, because our circumstances had been different. My son had anticipated what my reaction might be and had delayed coming out to us until he was no longer living at home. This meant that I was spared the complications of everyday contact and the inevitable urge to try and pressurise my son into "change". Nevertheless, I was shaken to realise the outcome that I might easily have faced under different circumstances. I also knew that if God had not shown up for Bobby's mother, or for all the others that I had read about, there was little reason to believe that he would show up for me.

Before I did any serious damage, I decided that discretion might be the better part of valour. I would let things be until such time as I could settle the confusion that was beginning to rage inside my head. This confusion struck at the core of my faith. *Prayers for Bobby* had a massive impact on my thinking and convinced me beyond all doubt that there must be something wrong, either with the Bible itself or at the very least with my (and other people's) understanding of it.

Peggy had also recommended that I read some books by Roberta Showalter Kreider. Roberta, whose husband had been a minister in both Mennonite and Brethren churches before his retirement, had discovered, late in life and just before her younger brother's death in 1984, that this younger brother had been gay. Her response, after the shock, was that she and her husband, in her words "*began listening to voices from the other side of the debate about homosexuality.*" This listening resulted in a large collection of stories from the LGBT community which Roberta edited and then published in three separate books. I shall return to these very important books in a later chapter.

A further useful book that Peggy recommended was titled *Homosexuality and Christian Faith,* containing articles contributed by various authors of differing Christian backgrounds, including one by Peggy Campolo herself. It is edited by Walter Wink, who is a Professor emeritus of Biblical interpretations at Auburn Theological Seminary in New York City, and it provides a different theological perspective from that taken by the overwhelming majority of evangelical Christians. This was useful in that it provided an approach to the Bible that did not necessarily exclude homosexuality in the scheme of things. Some of the authors claimed to be of evangelical persuasion themselves in that they accepted the Bible as the Word of God. Their interpretation of the Bible, however, is not likely to meet with much sympathy among the evangelicals with whom I am familiar.

The result of reading all this material is that my attitude to homosexuality underwent a fundamental change. I thought back to the time that our son had come out to us. Now the full force of his words came home to me: "*I [AM] gay.*" I had come to realise that being gay was not something he had chosen in preference to being heterosexual, but was rather an essential part of his make-up, an integral part of who he was. It was not some add-on to his personality, and it did not appear to be a changeable condition—looking back, I began to accept that it was something that had always been there. In short, my son was gay, he had always been gay and would always be gay and I would have to come to terms with that fact. This realisation presented my wife and I with the problem of our own coming out. We are still in this process as to date we have not found the courage to confide in all of our friends.

Part of the problem lies in the fact that parents cannot confide in others on this issue without this impinging on their child's privacy, and this is an immensely complicated business. It is, ultimately, the gay person's prerogative to decide who should know. Our son no longer lives with us and he has distanced himself from his growing-up years, but he is sensitive about the issue of people he grew up amongst now knowing that he is gay. As all parents will be aware, however, long term friends do have the habit of asking about your children and some will do so regularly, generally wishing to know if they have "*found anybody yet*." It is a normal part of life, a standard topic of conversation between parents who have children of a certain age, but not one that is particularly welcome when a problem of this nature surfaces.

Being forced into a position of endless deception to shield your child is uncomfortable to put it mildly, and is something that the child will not necessarily appreciate fully. When the issue concerns immediate family, it can be a huge problem. We had already told our closest relatives, as I had a gut feeling that my own family would be understanding or at least accepting. Both of us come from families that are very close-knit. In fact, my elder brother, a Canon in the Anglican Church, told me that he had a lesbian woman in his congregation, although he did not say if this was widely known in his church. My younger, rather worldlier brother (a term not used here in a derogatory sense), told us that he knew several gay or lesbian people and said it was "*just the way things are.*" My parents were both dead so I was spared that obstacle.

My wife had told her mother and sisters when she went for a holiday to Peru to visit them. Her mother was accepting, but her two sisters seemed unable to comprehend why anyone should "choose" to be gay and both still seem to think that "healing" is possible, a view that is fostered by the attitudes in the Catholic Church.

Beyond the immediate family, I decided to confide in the Pastor of the church that we attended. Deception in this area would seem to have been a denial of everything that I claimed to believe. In the event, as with many very large churches, the pastor, who had a global ministry, could no longer undertake to counsel individuals and I was referred to the senior assistant pastor.

I already knew the senior assistant pastor reasonably well, which helped, though I was somewhat surprised by the very sympathetic hearing he gave me. I was fully aware of the views expressed within the church from time to time, particularly by many of the visiting preachers who came. I had also heard one of two remarks that he himself had made when preaching that made me feel he was probably a homophobe. It is amazing how sensitive you can become to the slightest hint of homophobia when any remark is made that might reflect on one of your children. In the event, he listened with great patience for over an hour and a half without interrupting and only occasionally asking questions or making any comment.

At the end, he told me that there was someone in the church who had been a homosexual but appeared to have been cured and indeed was in a heterosexual marriage. I had heard of this person but never actually met him. He promised to read the various books that I left with him, including *Prayers for Bobby,* and said that he would arrange for me to meet with the "healed" gay man. He ended by giving me a hug and he was obviously concerned, if not a little perplexed, about what I had told him.

By the time the promised meeting took place I had a much deeper understanding of homosexuality, perhaps as much as it is possible for a non-homosexual to have. I certainly had enough understanding to know that the person with whom I was talking had definitely not been healed. One of the first things that he said to me, by way of introduction, was that he was not claiming that this was a "done deal". He had, he confessed, to be very vigilant, lest he be sucked back into this "abominable" lifestyle. The Bible, of course, refers to the practice of homosexuality as an abomination, at least in the King James Version.

Neither I, nor, I believe, any other heterosexual person has ever had to wake up in the morning worrying that they might get sucked into homosexual temptation. Anyone who does wake up with this fear is still struggling with homosexual tendencies and cannot claim to be healed. They are merely practising what psychologists refer to as behaviour control, which is a vastly different thing. I was harangued for nearly an hour for toying with the idea of "*buying into these lies of the devil,*" in other words for even thinking about accepting homosexual behaviour in my son or anybody else. My offer of a copy of the film *Prayers for Bobby* was refused with a wave of the hand and a comment about such stuff being filth.

He spoke with the zeal of a man who, I felt, had been thoroughly brainwashed, and who supposed that if he denounced homosexuals with sufficient passion, he would further distance himself from the problem. This is exactly what one gay pastor, who has told his story on the Courage UK website, did imagine. He became an anti-gay demagogue, or "gay-basher" in evangelical parlance, in the belief that it would help to make his own problem go away and save his marriage. It did not.

One of the leading lights in the ex-gay movement was a lesbian named Darlene Bogle. For more than ten years she was the principal female spokesperson for Exodus International and also directed her own venture, Paraklete Ministries, for helping lesbian women to become straight. She admits that she so sublimated her own desires and personality beneath a fanaticism for the ideology (or Christian doctrine) that she had embraced that she assumed she had been healed, or at least that the desires of same sex attraction had left her. Of course, she was wrong, but she did not realise this until she fell in love with another woman who had attended one of her conferences.

Clearly, it is possible to so immerse yourself in some cause or some crusade that you can forget who you really are because you do not give your real self any time for self-expression. It is one means of behaviour control, but it is still a very long way away from being healed. Darlene's courageous apology to all the lesbians that she mislead by imparting false information during her long, high profile ministry can be accessed via the *Courage UK* website. She admits that the question most frequently asked at her conferences was "*How long must I wait*?" The only answer she was ever able to offer was "*Be patient.*" A more honest answer would have been "*Forever*" but Darlene did not know this at the time.

The testimony of the "ex-gay" man in my own Church continued to be used in the training of young people preparing themselves for active and possibly full-time service in the church. It serves to bolster the claim of Bible infallibility and to demonstrate the power of belief in God's Word as well as to discredit those who advocate any lessening of clearly stated biblical standards.

The assistant pastor that I spoke to did eventually read *Prayers for Bobby* and also *Homosexuality and*

Christianity. He confessed that the Church leadership was not all of one mind regarding this issue and there had been some lively debate on the subject at times. This surprised and even encouraged me and I gave him another excellent DVD called *For the Bible Tells Me So*, which is a documentary about five sets of Christian parents who each discover that they have a gay child. Many weeks later, when he had still not got around to watching it, a further crisis erupted.

We had, by now, confided in one or two of our closest friends in the church. Some were supportive and one or two admitted to having gay or lesbian friends and even gay or lesbian relatives. However, one or two were far less accepting and warned us not to "*buy into the lies of the devil*" (a favourite phrase often used in the church), because homosexuality was an abomination in the eyes of God. My wife was deeply hurt by these comments and stopped attending church shortly afterwards. She had suffered from depressive tendencies for some time and there was a noticeable deterioration in her well-being. This experience of rejection also made both of us far more cautious about who we chose to confide in.

A few months later, for the sake of our marriage, I also stopped attending the church. At the time, as far as I knew, the film *For the Bible Tells Me So* had still not been watched. There were, no doubt, more pressing issues that needed to be dealt with, but for me it was an issue that had come to dominate my whole perspective.

Chapter 9   A FALSE IMAGE

Two other things occurred around this time. My image of a homosexual man was largely that of an effeminate person of the sort that used to be portrayed on the television. This, in spite of the fact that I had worked with several gay colleagues, none of whom conformed to this stereotypical image in any way. However, I then read a book, written by Esera Tuaolo, about his experiences as a gay man playing American football in the National Football League (NFL) at the very highest level. Titled *Alone in the Trenches*, it introduced me to a quite different image of a gay man. Here was someone who, by any standards, was a magnificent physical specimen, playing one of the most physically demanding of all sports, in an ultra-macho environment. Gay? Clearly, I would have to revise my preconceptions.

More recently, Gareth Thomas, the most capped Welsh Rugby Union player of all time and who captained both Wales and the British Lions, has also come out. Gareth was married for four years to his childhood sweetheart, an extremely pretty girl judging by her photograph in the newspapers. He was obviously very fond of her, but he is yet another person who apparently thought that being in a heterosexual marriage would in some way help him resolve his sexual conflicts. He was, sadly, wrong, and the consequences of being wrong are not confined to him alone. There are two people in a marriage and hence two lives that are deeply affected by mistakes such as this, not to mention the families of both parties.

One can only admire the tremendous courage and honesty of Gareth and the fortitude of his wife and hope that both will have happy and more satisfying futures. What should concern us is that these false notions, still held by many and propagated in evangelical (and Catholic) Christian circles, will encourage others to make the same, unnecessary mistake, with all the resulting heartache.

The second occurrence was meeting our son's boyfriend. We have always been a little apprehensive as well as excited when meeting our eldest son's girlfriends and our daughters' boyfriends for the first time, and this is natural. You want to like them and you want them to like you. So we were particularly apprehensive about this first meeting, as we had no information and no idea what to expect. As it turned out, the boyfriend was six feet three inches tall, very well built and among his favourite pastimes was shootfighting, which apparently is some form of mixed martial arts.

My wife later commented that there must be thousands of single girls around who would die for a boyfriend as handsome as he was. To our immense relief, we genuinely did like him, and we could not help but notice how much happier our son was and how much easier it was for us to communicate with him as a result of this relationship. With this meeting, we had, in one sense, completed a major part of our journey. Not only had we come to accept our son's sexual orientation, but we could finally be happy for him, happy that he was now free to pursue his own happiness in life.

All our children are precious to us and their happiness is of paramount importance. My son's homosexuality does not mean that he is in any way odd or inadequate or sinful, in wilful defiance of his Creator's wishes, as once I might have thought. He is simply a young man who is attracted to members of the same sex. In all other respects, he is just like I am. I cannot pretend to understand this as a heterosexual but at least I am now able to accept it. What happens between any two people in private is not my concern. As long as their behaviour does no harm to others then I cannot see what it has to do with anyone but themselves.

The thought of heterosexuals imagining that they have some right to interfere in the private lives of those who do not happen to be heterosexuals is something that I find somewhat offensive. To do so under the guise of protecting the morality of the nation, or from some notion of occupying a God-given position of higher morality than the rest of the unbelieving world, I now find very offensive. I even find it offensive for people to claim that this is a Christian nation and that they are upholding Christian standards, as if Christianity itself should be beyond question. I am aware that Christianity has moulded the nation's beliefs and moral values for a millennium and a half and that these beliefs and values are ingrained in many of us; they are a part of our heritage, our culture. I, as much as anybody, am aware that the Christian gospel has had an enormous influence for good in many different ways. None of this, however, has any bearing on the validity of Christian beliefs or moral standards. And none of it gives the Christian world the right to victimise and condemn any minority group, especially a group of whose problems they clearly have so little understanding.

Scientific knowledge has done away with a lot of misconceptions that once were held to be obvious truths, such as the Earth being at the centre of the universe, a belief that had the sanction of the Catholic Church. Religious "truth" needs to be subjected to the same scrutiny as any other branch of knowledge. If it is found to be at odds with the best scientific knowledge available, and its adherents cannot provide any evidence to support their views other than "*God says in the Bible*" or "*The Qur'ân says,*" then perhaps the time has come to insist homosexuals should be regarded as innocent unless, at some future date, greater knowledge can conclusively demonstrate that they are, after all, guilty. Fortunately, in Britain at least, this attitude is becoming more and more the norm. However, having lived in two developing countries for lengthy periods, I cannot help but be concerned at the obvious, and unfortunately damaging, influence that evangelical Christianity is having in these countries when it comes to attitudes towards homosexuality.

Moral values would seem to be based on nothing more than what the majority of human beings find acceptable. That is why they change with time and also from culture to culture. The idea that there are absolute values that are sanctioned by God and have been revealed by him to one or two special individuals has no evidence to support it and the very notion of this seems ridiculous at the dawn of a new millennium.

Chapter 10   REPARATIVE THERAPY

Reparative therapy seems to be a general term for therapies based on the ideas of Dr. Elizabeth Moberly, usually credited with being the originator of gender-affirmative therapy. Dr. Moberly's ideas are contained in a short book published in 1983, titled *Homosexuality: A New Christian Ethic.* The influence of this book on the world of evangelical Christianity has been enormous and is out of all proportion to its content. In all my reading of evangelical literature, when writers seek support from sources other than the Bible for their own views on homosexuality, she is the most widely quoted author by some distance,

Therefore, it is worthwhile to take a look at the claims made in Dr. Moberly's book. The first disconcerting fact it is that details of the author's specific qualifications for writing such a book are not provided. We are merely informed that it was written during a period of Guest Membership at Lucy Cavendish College, Cambridge. I have made a number of attempts to find out exactly what field her PhD might be in, searching the Internet and contacting people who claim to have known her, and also the publishers of her book, but all to no avail.

Jeffry G. Ford, a licensed psychologist and a gay Christian, at whose house Dr. Moberly apparently stayed on one of her visits to the USA, refers to her as a "*British theologian and self-proclaimed psychologist*" in an article on his website which condemns reparative therapy. He and a number of others had received Dr.

Moberly's ideas with great enthusiasm when they were first propounded. It took a number of years before disillusionment set in and he felt obliged to abandon his efforts. He now refers to reparative therapy as a pseudo-science. I cannot comment on his statement about Dr. Moberly's qualifications but I do think that book companies should have a duty to provide relevant information about people whose books they choose to publish, especially when the contents of the book might be described as controversial and are such that they may adversely affect the lives of particular groups of people within society. Sadly, in this instance and for reasons only known to themselves, the publishers saw fit not to do so.

The book itself purports to offer a new explanation of the causes of homosexuality and then to offer a new line of treatment for a "cure". However, her work appears to be based entirely on a reappraisal of previous literature on the subject. She makes no mention of any experience of her own in counselling gay or lesbian people. What she does do is to make some quite staggering claims, given the circumstances. At the end of chapter 2, she writes: "*It is only a true understanding of the problem that can lead to its true solution. Healing for the homosexual is entirely possible—but it has not yet genuinely been tried!*"

First, there is an admission in this statement that there was no previous record of any successful "treatment" for homosexuality; if there had been there would be no need for her book. Second, there is the claim that a hitherto untried treatment will provide the "healing" that is deemed necessary. This is followed by two chapters of more specifically Christian perspective, before the book ends with the claim "*If we are willing to seek and meditate the healing and redeeming love of Christ, then healing for the homosexual will become a great and glorious reality.*"

Such claims, which do not appear to be based on any substantiated evidence, would seem to be rather extravagant in 1983 when the book was first published. There followed seven reprints with the original publishers, James Clarke & Co, between 1985 and 2001, and a further reprint in 2006 with their sister imprint, The Lutterworth Press, who claim to specialise in high quality Christian books. This last reprint was twenty-three years after the first publication. One might expect that a book which made such serious and spectacular claims in 1983 would have been updated in the intervening twenty-three years to include some evidence of the effectiveness of the treatment that had been proposed. You cannot go on forever claiming that the correct treatment has not yet genuinely been tried. It has been tried, and in most cases, and quite probably all cases, found wanting. It appears to maintain credibility only in specifically religious circles where there is a clear vested interest in the "success" of this type of therapy.

I phoned The Lutterworth Press and was allowed to speak with the managing director, who listened politely to my concerns about this book. I asked him why his company was reprinting such a dated book which by now contained some patently false statements. He was exceedingly courteous but replied that Dr. Moberly was quite entitled to her opinions. What I suspect he really meant was that it makes sense to reprint any book if there is still demand for it and hence it is likely to make money.

Obviously, her book is still in demand by the evangelical fraternity because it says exactly what they wish to believe. To his credit, he offered to forward a letter from myself to Dr. Moberly, "*providing he could find her address.*" In this letter I simply asked if she herself had had any definite evidence of the efficacy of her therapy in the intervening years since she first made her claims. I do not know whether she ever received my letter but I do know that I never received any reply. This experience was the first concrete occasion that I felt I had been subject to evasion and a certain amount of hypocrisy in the evangelical world. It was certainly not to be the last.

Chapter 11 MORE QUESTIONABLE LITERATURE

My brush with The Lutterworth Press was soon to be followed by a similar experience with the Inter-Varsity Press (ivp). Their books have had, and still do have, a major influence on the evangelical movement in Britain. I had read many of them in my time at university and afterwards. The Christian Union ran a book stall stocked almost entirely with their books and local evangelical churches often did likewise.

Now, however, I read a book titled *Walking with Gay Friends* by a lesbian Christian girl, Alex Tylee, which had been published in 2007. I found this book to be very disturbing. The author appeared to me to be deeply unhappy about her situation and seemed to be sustained only by an assumption that "*I serve a God who could most certainly change my sexual orientation enough for me to have as happy and godly a marriage as anyone*" (Page 27). She is clearly aided and abetted in this (almost certainly false) assumption by her Christian friends and by those in charge of ivp publications. Such a view, totally unsupported by any concrete evidence, is not only dubious but is also very dangerous. Bobby Griffith committed suicide with views similar to this no doubt ringing in his head.

People who are closely involved with counselling teenagers with sexual identity problems apparently find that many contemplate suicide. Of course, many teenagers commit suicide for unknown reasons, although depression and bullying appear to be among the common causes. People who are different, however, are more likely to be bullied and difference can often be accentuated by issues of a sexual nature. Even if specific reasons for many teenage suicides are not known, it is not unreasonable to suggest that sexual identity problems may play a significant role. This being the case, responsible people ought not to aggravate an already difficult issue by promoting contentious opinions regarding issues of human sexuality, particularly when such claims are made on nothing more substantial than religious belief.

Alex Tylee also quotes the views of Dr. Moberly as if these were the scientific views of an acknowledged expert in the field. Dr. Moberly's opinions, however, are disputed by the Royal College of Psychiatrists who state in their report *Submission to the Church of England's Listening Exercise* on Human Sexuality that "*Although there is now a number of therapists and organisation [sic] in the USA and the UK that claim that therapy can help homosexuals to become heterosexual, there is no evidence that such change is possible.*" The report is available on the Internet. Dr. Moberly's support appears to be confined to professional bodies that exist to cater for members with evangelical protestant, Roman Catholic or possibly Mormon beliefs, which are given precedence over mainline medical or scientific opinion. The membership of such institutions is very small compared to the membership of the main professional institutions that are not circumscribed by religious belief, but which, nevertheless, must contain a number of members with religious convictions.

The book also carries a ringing endorsement on its back cover from Dr. Justin Thacker who is the Head of

Theology at the Evangelical Alliance. In a previous life he was a medical doctor with a speciality in paediatrics. Among the book's many supposed qualities, Dr. Thacker includes "informed" and says that it is "*evangelicalism at its best.*" Dr. Thacker appears to take the word "informed" to mean "in complete agreement with the evangelical party line." I have come across quite a lot of genuine information on homosexuality that is not mentioned in this "informed" treatise. It is, no doubt, evangelicalism at its best because this is what evangelicalism is best at: presenting dubious and often uninformed opinions as probable fact for dissemination to the faithful.

After a long association with this movement I have been driven to the conclusion that even the most educated among its membership find it difficult, if not impossible, to free themselves from the slavery of their own prejudices. Thus they demonstrate that they are ordinary members of the human race and not Holy Spirit-inspired members of another world.

I sent a copy of the film *Prayers for Bobby* to the managing director of the Inter-Varsity Press and suggested that at least he should watch it so that he could be fully aware of the possible consequences of the type of literature that his organisation was publishing. I also said that I would be very grateful to receive any comments on the film that he may have. I further included a letter addressed to Alex Tylee and asked if he would be willing to forward the letter to her. I received no reply from any quarter. It became apparent that in the world of evangelical Christians, consequences for individuals, however tragic, do not matter. Purity of doctrine and faith are of the essence.

If people choose to sin, then they must be prepared to accept the consequences. Thus, they absolve themselves from all responsibility.

There are certain high-sounding statements that, having been made by someone, become part and parcel of the evangelical world. One such statement is the following: "*I do not condemn homosexuals, but I cannot condone the lifestyle that they have chosen to live.*" Such a statement first contains a disclaimer: "*I am not guilty of bigotry. In fact I consider myself to have a very enlightened and sympathetic view of the homosexual's problems, but . . . .*" We then find the word "*chosen*", which could be interpreted to mean that they think that anyone who is homosexual should "choose" to remain celibate, presumably so that heterosexual sensibilities might not be offended. However, there is the real belief among the majority of evangelicals that homosexuals actually choose to be homosexuals in preference to being heterosexuals. Surprisingly few people bother to stop and ask themselves if they, on reaching puberty, ever made any conscious choice as to whether they would be attracted to people of the opposite sex as opposed to those of the same sex.

Evangelicals are also quite adept at hinting that some homosexuals have been healed and they appear to require little or no evidence in order to make these claims. Hearsay seems perfectly acceptable as long as it serves the purpose of supporting the beliefs they hold. Indeed many have been encouraged to testify to their healing very soon after they have received prayer to this end. What you never hear evangelicals admit is the number of people who, at some later date, suffer a relapse into having homosexual feelings and possibly back into homosexual activity. Nobody needs to look very far to find that such people are plentiful. Bad news is buried and forgotten. There are always, as someone has remarked, newly "healed" people who can be paraded before the faithful. It is a shabby exercise in deceit and hypocrisy, but who cares if the end justifies the means—the end being the unqualified affirmation of the inspiration and inerrancy of the Bible?

I was a part of the evangelical world for forty years. It is a world where people are welcome only as long as they follow the leadership and ask no awkward questions. After all, no brother can expect any blessing from God if he doubts the Word of God. Such a brother is no brother at all and should be cut off totally. Better that he be handed over to Satan, to be taught not to blaspheme—a fate suffered by Hymeneals and Alexander at the hands of St. Paul in 1 Timothy 1:20. I was tempted to be politically correct and put he/she for the pronoun (third word in the previous sentence) until I remembered that Paul would not have dreamed of having any dialogue with a woman over any religious issue. The crux of the matter is that the whole point of faith is to have unquestioning belief without any need for proof.

Chapter 12 THE "LISTENING" ANGLICAN CHURCH

While I was engaged in my own search for truth regarding homosexuality, the Anglican Church was preparing for another of its ten-yearly Lambeth Conferences for bishops in the worldwide Anglican Communion. The issue of homosexuality had been, for some considerable time, both very prominent and extremely divisive in this organisation and it was clear that the topic was going to occupy a central place in their deliberations once again.

The first mention of the issue of homosexuality at these conferences appears to be in resolution 10 of the 1978 conference which recognised the "*need for a deep and dispassionate study of the issue of homosexuality, which would take seriously both the teaching of Scripture and the results of scientific and medical research.*" In the conference of 1988, ten years later, resolution 64 reaffirmed resolution 10 from the 1978 conference but now linked homosexuality to the issue of human rights. Other than that, there seemed to have been no concrete progress in this ten year interval.

In the 1998 conference, resolution 1:10 committed the Communion to "*listen to the experience of homosexual persons*" although at the same it recognised "*homosexual practice as incompatible with Scripture.*" Once again there seemed to be no concrete progress, unless the inference that homosexual practice is unacceptable is taken as an unequivocal condemnation, which it clearly is. After all, it is the practice of homosexuality that is the issue. Homosexuality that is not expressed can hardly be offensive to anybody.

Prior to the 2008 conference, the Communion was urged by the Vatican to issue a clear rejection of homosexuality. In an extremely long report that was of a different style to previous reports, there did not seem to be any resolutions as such but instead 162 statements that tried to reflect the "*general substance and flavour of the conference.*" Statements 105 to 120, under Section H, are to do with human sexuality.

Having read through all this, the impression that I was left with was one of total confusion. It virtually amounts to a frank admission that the issue was one of such complexity that it was beyond their power, and by implication, beyond God's power, to resolve it. So, like any good political party, they opted for a policy of more procrastination. Maybe the problem would go away if they continued to ignore it. However, what had seemed a peripheral issue in 1978 had clearly been allowed to grow into one of major importance and giant complexity in the intervening thirty years. The statement ends with twelve suggestions for possible ways forward. The last of these was to "*Declare a 'Decade of Sharing and Generosity' and keep walking, keep talking, keep listening together.*" In other words, more of what had proved totally unproductive over the previous thirty years.

It is interesting to know that a documentary film, *For the Bible Tells Me So*, was sent to the 2008 conference (not by me!) for the enlightenment of the assembled bishops. I have been informed that it was an optional item on the conference agenda and that a significant number of bishops refused to watch it. If true, it is probably not surprising, since the parents of Gene Robinson, the gay Anglican bishop whose consecration was a major cause of disunity in the Church, were among the parents featured. Bishop Robinson himself was at first invited to attend the conference but his invitation was withdrawn when it became obvious that his presence was likely to be a cause of considerable tension.

The refusal of some bishops to watch the film indicates the extent of the bigotry involved. It amounts to a statement that they had made up their minds and were not prepared to be influenced by any evidence. One might have more respect for such bishops if they had watched the film and then offered some reasoned rejection of its message. As in the case of Bobby Griffith, there features an account of a harrowing suicide, this time that of a lesbian girl, Anna Wallner, whose own mother's inability to accept her daughter's sexuality was a major factor in the tragic outcome.

The real issue, to any observant outsider, has actually changed focus; it is no longer primarily about homosexuality but rather about the Church's credibility. In fact, the Anglican Church has been involved in what has been a great spiritual experiment, lasting more than thirty years, involving its claim to divine guidance. If you read the literature that has been put out by the Anglican Church on this topic, you will notice that little phrases such as "*led by the Spirit*" are inserted to bolster the credibility of their deliberations. If, after thirty years of walking, talking, sharing, listening, discussing, possibly fasting and presumably praying, there is no evidence whatsoever of any clear leading from the Holy Spirit, then the Holy Spirit must have questionable interest in the affairs of the Anglican Church, or, a much less palatable conclusion, the Holy Spirit is nothing more than an invention of the religious imagination. The rest of us, in any case, could be forgiven for imagining that the Holy Spirit has been supplanted by humbug in all these deliberations.

It could, of course, be the case that the Holy Spirit has been speaking, but that perhaps not all of the bishops have been listening. If that is the case, there does not seem to be any way of knowing which bishops are the guilty ones, except for those Bishops with evangelical/fundamentalist leanings who know that it is the "others" who are spiritually deaf.

Whatever the truth, the Anglican Church clearly cares more about an appearance of unity than it does about the lives of any homosexuals, because while the bishops go on prevaricating, the Bobby Griffiths and the Anna Wallners of this world will go on committing suicide. That, to my mind, and no doubt the minds of many others, is a price that is just too high. It will be the price of mindboggling incomprehension and incompetence in a Church that refuses to acknowledge the disastrous consequences that its indecision is having on many of the young and maybe the not so young members of our society. What an indictment of a Church to say that it cares more about Church unity than it does about human tragedy.

Anyone who has read section H of the report on the conference will probably be struck by an attempt to camouflage its vacuity under a welter of pious prose and sanctimonious spirituality. It is the typical product of the deliberations of a committee—a very large committee in this case and one that does not give the impression that it was involved with an issue of such gravitas. It would be instructive to compare the activities of the bishops with those of the two gay pastors mentioned previously, Mel White and Anthony Venn-Brown. They certainly could not be faulted for any lack of effort in their respective attempts to find a solution to their problem. How would this contrast with the wining and dining that almost certainly punctuated the meetings and general discussions of the people who continue to pronounce judgement on the Mels, Anthonys, Bobbys and Annas in our midst?

I am not trying to minimise the difficulties that this particular issue does cause. A movement with a worldwide membership will inevitably encounter problems with different cultural attitudes. However, cultural attitudes have nothing to do with truth. The function of those in responsible positions in the Church hierarchy is to hear the truth from God and then, if necessary, set about educating the membership so that a change of mind regarding particular issues can be brought about. This requires the Church to be certain about what it believes and then to speak with a clear voice.

When the leadership does not know where the truth lies, it will inevitably resort to canvassing public opinion as to what is acceptable or pragmatic or even possible. Instead of leading, it will allow itself to be led by circumstances. It is impossible to avoid the impression that this is exactly what is happening in an Anglican Church that does not know where the truth lies because it has not heard from God on this issue and therefore, in all probability, has never heard from God on any issue. It is a Church that is simply being reluctantly dragged along in the wake of public opinion, but is a very long way behind that opinion.

The great problem with any listening exercise is that people only hear what they want to hear; they listen for confirmation of their existing beliefs, not for the purpose of enlightenment. The idea that anything useful will emerge from all this listening is based on false ideas of the human psyche. It is far more likely that entrenched positions will become even more entrenched. An old English proverb highlights the problem very succinctly: "*A man convinced against his will, is of the same opinion still.*" People will believe what they want to believe, irrespective of the likelihood of there being any truth associated with their beliefs.

Max Planck, the great German physicist, is regarded as the father of a theory that revolutionised his subject in the twentieth century, namely quantum theory. An English rendering of what he wrote in his autobiography is as follows: "*A new scientific truth does not triumph by convincing its opponents and making them see the light; rather its opponents eventually die and a new generation emerges that is more familiar with the ideas.*" That is an admission that even the most intelligent of people in this world find it exceedingly difficult to change their opinions once those opinions, or beliefs, have been held for any length of time. Planck was writing about the world of science. Perhaps its counterpart in the world of religion is exemplified by the Anglican Church.

In 2018, the Anglican Church will hold its next Lambeth Conference. It will then be a biblical forty years since it first began to worry about the problem of homosexuality. Forty years is the period of time that the Israelites are said to have wandered in the desert after leaving Egypt and before they entered the Promised Land. The reason for this extraordinarily long interval was to allow an entire generation of fighting men, whose courage had failed them at a crucial moment and who had refused to rally to Joshua and Caleb and take the land of Canaan by conquest, to die off and be replaced by another generation not beset with the same fears (Numbers 14:21-23).

Perhaps the Anglican Church is hoping that forty years will allow a new generation of bishops to take office, a generation of bishops not beset with the limited and befuddled vision of a number of its predecessors, a generation more willing to take on board the findings of medical science, a generation that will finally be able to come to one mind as to what "*the Spirit is saying.*" By then, of course, public opinion may have moved so much that no pronouncement by the Church on this issue will any longer be of relevance. People without the "leading of the Spirit" may well have ushered in a new age of enlightenment. A less charitable explanation is that a policy of procrastination lets the present generation of bishops off the hook and leaves the mess to its successors.

One voice that the Anglican Church does not appear to be interested in listening to is that of Desmond Tutu, the retired Archbishop of Cape Town, South Africa. He is a man who was well accustomed to being discriminated against on account of something beyond his control—in his case the colour of his skin. I once heard him say in a radio interview something along the following lines:

"*To think that anyone would deliberately choose to belong to a minority group of people who are often hated, ridiculed, despised, persecuted and shunned, is ridiculous.*" He expresses similar sentiments on the DVD *For the Bible Tells Me So.*

Another voice that they could listen to with benefit is that of (the late) Frankie Howerd, who was a popular, gay, British comedian. Cilla Black (a well-known British singer/TV personality), says that he told her on one occasion that if he could take a pill that would alter his sexuality, he would take it that same day. She found that to be very sad, as indeed it was. Such a wish was not that of a man who had chosen to be gay. I have never come across any convincing account of a person who chose to be gay. Nobody chooses their sexuality. Many come to accept their sexuality because, in the end, they have no choice. That, however, is a million miles away from what is believed by huge numbers of religious people, Jews, Christians and Muslims alike.

Chapter 13 EVIDENCE FROM LGBT CHRISTIANS

During the period following the Lambeth Conference, while I was engaged in trying to correspond with several known conservative Anglican bishops and other senior figures, I was also reading numerous accounts of the experiences of specifically Christian people in the LGBT community. Many of these had been compiled by Roberta Showalter Kreider and published in three books: *From Wounded Hearts* (1998; second edition 2003); *Together In Love* (2002) and *The Cost of Truth* (2004). They are hugely important because, to my knowledge, they provide the only really extensive collection of such accounts that exists. They are, therefore, an excellent reference source for anyone who seriously wishes to become more informed.

The accounts have been gathered from a limited field, mostly, though not exclusively, from members of the Mennonite and Brethren denominations and particularly from people living in the state of Pennsylvania. The fact that she was able to compile so many of these accounts just serves to show how many LGBT Christians there may be.

The accounts are varied, some uplifting, some sad and tragic, but all stories of real people who had to face real issues and serious difficulties that were not of their own choosing. Indeed, many found their choices in life greatly restricted by the reaction of others once the issue of their sexuality came to light. People who had entertained aspirations of Christian service could find themselves marginalised or ignored at best but sometimes ostracised or totally rejected by the churches in which they had grown up and sometimes by their own families. Even the stories that could be said to have happy endings had invariably included much hardship and heartache along the way, something that would not have occurred in a more comprehending and compassionate society. The elevation of biblical dogma above these virtues in many Christian circles is a sad indictment of their priorities.

As I read stories of shattered dreams and ruined lives among these accounts, I felt a new emotion being aroused within me. It was one of anger. What right did Anglican Bishops or the Pope or anybody else have to condemn such people? What did they know of the struggles, the frustrations or the heartaches that these people had to endure? How many of them had ever heard of Roberta Showalter Kreider, much less read any of her books? I began to feel that most of them knew very little and cared even less.

In not one of these accounts did I read of anyone who had deliberately chosen to be homosexual in preference to being heterosexual. Instead, I was reading story after story of people who entered a world of confusion, a world that frightened them, a world from which they wished they could escape, and in almost every case tried desperately hard to do so. Many sought prayer; many were prayed for by highly regarded church leaders and evangelists at various conferences, but were to discover that when these prayers had no effect they were made to feel unwelcome.

As a teacher, I was aware that young people first and foremost want to belong. They want to be accepted by their peers, to be the same as everyone else. People growing up rarely make a conscious decision to be different, unless they are extremely talented and supremely confident. Differences tend to emerge when ordinary people are made to feel different, when they are excluded and made to feel that somehow they do not belong and are not wanted.

I thought back to the claim of the Anglican churches to be engaged in a listening exercise. Who were they listening to? Roberta Showalter Kreider and her husband did not seem to have encountered insurmountable obstacles in their search. I did not encounter undue difficulties in my search. I found a huge number of people to listen to, either in books or articles on the Internet, particularly at the *Courage UK* website. There was no shortage of witnesses—more than enough to make any rational, honest person pause and ask some serious questions.

Why, therefore, should some of the bishops in the Anglican Church find it so hard to listen? How can they claim, as they do by implication, that there is insufficient evidence to come to any definite conclusion, even after 30 years? How many of them know about Bobby Griffith or Anna Wallner or any other gay or lesbian person whose story has been recorded to inform those who wish to listen? Listening, as I have discovered, is a highly selective process. Too often we choose to listen to those with whose views we already concur.

Roy Clements is a gay evangelical Christian. He was once a very successful Baptist minister, a married man with children and an extremely popular speaker on the evangelical conference circuit. Having attended many similar conferences, I know that his messages would have been listened to avidly, and they would have been regarded as *"God's word for today."* As the evangelicals became increasingly homophobic in outlook, however, he felt forced to confront his own sexual leanings and voice his dissent, something that is not tolerated in the evangelical world. His fall from grace was instant. He was ostensibly given sabbatical leave to sort out his problems, but in reality he appears to have been cast aside in a most shabby fashion. Very few people from the evangelical world showed any interest in "listening" to his story and, as far as I can gather, most never bothered to make contact with him again.

Roy seems to have committed the unpardonable sin of crossing sides. The hero had turned traitor in a highly charged game of politics, a game where any objective search for truth and understanding is subordinated to the more important issue of fighting for the entrenched position, struggling on behalf of the cause—the cause, in this case, being the preservation of biblical authority with regard to its moral teachings. Serious consequences for real people can be swept aside in the interests of doctrinal purity. Evangelicals seem psychologically unable to cope with people who "defect" for whatever reason. It seems that they can only protect their own (insecure) faith by banishing the thought of problem people from their minds. Perhaps, however, their attitudes are driven by a saying of Jesus: *"No-one who puts his hand to the plough and looks back is fit for service in the kingdom of God"* (Luke 9:62). If Jesus himself demonstrated intolerance in this area, it is perhaps not so surprising that his followers do so.

Roberta's books raised another, very worrying issue for me. Of the seven Bible references to homosexuality, one purports to offer an explanation for its existence. In Romans 1:18-27, a letter attributed to St. Paul, we are told that it occurred because God had abandoned people to this perversion on account of the fact that they did not acknowledge him or give him the worship that was his due. That explanation was in complete conflict with a great deal of what I had just been reading. If it was true, then surely it should mean that homosexuality ought to be found only among unbelievers? This, however, is clearly far from the case. Homosexuality is by no means unknown among the children of evangelical families. Ex-gay ministries in the USA have no shortage of young people being enrolled on their courses by frantic Christian parents, persuaded by the dubious, if not totally false, claims that are made for the effects of the "therapy" on offer.

In short, Paul's explanation must be wrong, and hence the Bible itself is wrong and is not an infallible guide even in the realm of morals. Because he had no real knowledge about human sexuality and hence could not offer any rational explanation, it had to be a religious problem. In ancient times, all problems with no known explanation were attributed to the anger of the Gods due to various shortcomings, intransigence or rebellion on the part of mankind. What other explanation could they offer?

Paul's explanation of homosexuality was, to me, a critical issue. It led me to the conclusion that he had no more access to divine inspiration than anybody else who might have been living at the time. It demonstrates that the Bible is not inspired in the way that evangelicals claim it to be. In fact, the Bible contains other, similar examples of patently false explanations, some of which are discussed in my follow-up book *Homosexuality: The Bible on Trial.*

The more I read, the more I was aware that I was beginning to think the unthinkable. Could it be that not only was the Bible not the inerrant Word of God that I had previously believed it to be, but in fact was not the Word of God in any sense at all? How could all these accounts of the desperate struggles of so many people, all from Christian families, be squared with what the Bible seemed to teach? And why did there seem to be such evasion and hypocrisy among those most prominent in proclaiming their faith when it came to dealing honestly with such important issues? Why such seeming lack of integrity, particularly in the ex-gay movements, when boasting of healings that, in most if not all cases, could not stand up to public scrutiny?

I was quite alarmed. Could all these people be the ones among whom I had spent so many happy times for forty years of my life? The truth that I had long been searching for did not seem to be leading me to where I had expected it to, or, indeed, to where I had wanted to go. But truth, in the end, however undesirable I might find it, had to be more important than my beliefs.

Chapter 14   MORE FRUSTRATION

Shortly before the Lambeth Conference of 2008, I had written to one or two Anglican bishops, and also the Archbishop of Canterbury, and sent copies of Leroy Adam's book, *Prayers for* Bobby, to each of them. I explained that I had a gay son and that issues regarding homosexuality were of some concern to me. I was not aware at the time that a film dealing with homosexuality, *For the Bible Tells Me So*, had also been sent to the conference to help enlighten the bishops with some concrete facts as they affect the parents of homosexual children. In truth, I had discovered *Prayers for Bobby* too late for it to be of much use to the bishops as they would have had little time to read it. I had been anxious to know how they could justify an interpretation of the Bible that led directly to the tragic outcome of Bobby's suicide at the age of twenty.

Later on I wrote to several more bishops and other leading figures in the Anglican establishment. When a film based on the book became available, I substituted this for the book because people who had little time to read books could surely find 90 minutes, even while eating a meal, to watch a film. I asked the same question of each of them: how could they endorse an interpretation of the Bible that led to such tragic loss of life? The response (or the lack of response in some cases) that I received from all this is revealing.

Michael Nazir-Ali, who was, at the time, Bishop of Rochester and in all probability the most conservative

Anglican bishop in England, replied with a personal, gracious letter, intended to be helpful. He dealt with several points that I had raised, but unfortunately it was clear that he had not read the book as he "*hoped that I had managed to find Christian counselling for my Son.*" Christian counselling appears to have been one of the things that ultimately contributed to Bobby's suicide.

I replied to this letter and received another long, personal letter in return, together with copies of talks that he had given on the topic. I was certainly appreciative of the time the bishop had given to me as I was someone that he did not know and had no direct responsibility towards, but I was disappointed that he would not address the central issue directly. Many of his views also appeared to be those of Dr. Moberly, a fact that he did not deny when I pointed this out to him, though he claimed that she was not his only source of reference.

I grant that bishops are busy under the best of circumstances and that he would have been particularly busy as he was on the point of immediate retirement from the position he held; perhaps he genuinely could not find the time to read the book. Regrettably, there will always remain the suspicion that he did not think the book worth reading as his mind was already firmly made up. If he has subsequently read the book out of curiosity, he has not let me know of any opinions he may have.

To the Reverend Dr. John Stott,* certainly one of the most influential people that the evangelical movement has ever known and whose books had influenced me in my early days as an evangelical Christian, I sent both the book and a copy of the film. He also gave me the courtesy of a personal reply, dictated to his secretary, explaining that he was now retired, in failing health and with failing eyesight, and that he could not read or watch television. However, he expressed his sympathy for my situation and recommended that I try to read his book *Issues Facing Christians Today,* as his views had been expressed in that book and that he felt there was nothing more he wished to add.

It did cross my mind that he could have asked one of his many visitors to read the book to him if he had had the remotest interest in this tragic story and the serious issues that it raises. I had already read his book once, some time ago, and was well aware of Dr. Stott's earlier views on the matter. However the book had undergone further editions, the latest being in 2006. It was rather disappointing therefore, to find that in the section dealing with homosexuality, the views of Dr. Moberly were still being quoted. There did not seem to be much point in pursuing this matter in view of Dr. Stott's circumstances. He had already more or less admitted that there was no evidence that could possibly cause him to have second thoughts.

From the Bishop of Winchester, the Rt. Revd. Michael Scott-Joint, another arch-conservative, I received a hand-written reply on a post card, thanking me for the book and saying that he would read it if he could find the time to do so, and if he did he would get back to me. The personal touch was appreciated. I subsequently sent him a copy of the film but unfortunately I never heard anything more from him.

The Archbishop of York, Dr. John Sentamu, is someone I know personally from the days when he was a student in Uganda, although he was not somebody that I ever actually taught. Because of this connection, I wrote several letters to him as well as sending him a copy of the book and film. He eventually sent a personal response but did not say much except that he had read the book and watched the film but he felt that matters could not be rushed and that the Church would have to be patient and await the Spirit's leading. The Holy Spirit, unfortunately, seems to be waiting to see which way public opinion will go before he offers any guidance of his own.

A number of other bishops replied via their diocesan office to acknowledge receipt of the book or film and in some cases recommended that I read material already written by the bishop on the subject. The diocesan office for the Bishop of Durham (Tom Wright at the time) replied that, as the bishop regularly worked a sixteen hour day, it was unlikely that he would find time to watch the film. What I read between the lines was that the issue seemed to be one of low priority, despite the fact that it seemed to be tearing his Church apart. Perhaps he should heed the advice of Jethro, Moses' father-in-law, recorded in Exodus 18:17-23. Jethro advised Moses that he was trying to carry too great a burden and needed to learn to delegate some of his responsibility.

Others that I knew personally, such as missionaries or Christian friends from my time in Uganda, did watch the film and replied to me, although not necessarily sympathetically in every case. Nevertheless, better an honest difference of opinion regarding the evidence than a refusal to acknowledge the existence of the evidence.

Still others did not even deign to reply, including the prominent evangelist Jay John, who is attached to the Anglican Church and who had visited the church that I used to attend on two or three occasions. I had reminded him of our very brief meeting on one of these occasions. The overwhelming impression that I got from all this is that many senior people within the Anglican Church had minds set in concrete and were not even willing to consider that there might be another perspective. So much for their "Listening Exercise." Not that this is a position peculiar to the Anglican Church. It is the default position of the majority of evangelicals and all fundamentalists everywhere and, indeed, of the Roman Catholic Church.

This whole experience left me feeling more and more alienated from those with whom I had once felt "*of one heart and mind.*" No longer did I see people of integrity, concerned solely with the truth. I rather saw closed minds whose agenda was to champion biblical dogma because they had made a prior decision to believe that the entire Bible was a revelation from God and hence beyond discussion. Of course I am aware of the conservative tendencies in many human beings and realise that few, if any, would greet the idea of rocking a boat that has sailed for two thousand years with glee, particularly when they are in that boat and they may have nowhere else to live. Tradition, too, is like a giant tree with enormous roots that is planted by the water side. Tradition is much harder to move than the mountain Jesus referred to in the Gospels seemed to be.

I had realised, by now, that any hope of a reassessment of the Bible teachings on homosexuality, as far as evangelicals were concerned, was completely misplaced. You cannot, unfortunately, reason with evangelical Christians on certain issues because they insist on basing their arguments on unverifiable assumptions and they refuse to acknowledge the existence of any evidence that they suspect might challenge their present beliefs. They are people, in general, with tunnel vision, closed minds and an inflexible agenda. In the end, the only way that the Anglican Church could ever resolve its dilemma with homosexuality and also maintain unity is to give in to the evangelicals. And now I realised that to maintain any integrity in my own life, I would have to cut my moorings loose and renounce the evangelical Christian world in which I had lived for so long.

* The Rev. Dr. John Stott, referred to in this chapter, died peacefully in July 2011, aged 90, shortly after I had finished writing the first draft of the book.

Chapter 15   QUESTIONS RAISED BY ISLAM

At the time that I embraced evangelical Christianity, most people in the English speaking world had little experience, or knowledge, of any religion other than Christianity. I certainly did not. Things have changed over the last forty years and we are all very well aware that Islam is an alternative, major religion and a force to be reckoned with in the modern world.

During my last years at school, I gave a sixth form general studies course that I called Science and Religion. I had volunteered to do this as I thought it would help in my quest to clarify my own mind about several issues, one of which was the matter of how far science and religion were, or were not, compatible with each other. I was to learn a great deal from this exercise.

The course seemed to attract a number of Muslim students. These students were all above average intelligence and some were very bright. Nevertheless, it was soon apparent that, despite their education and desire to learn science as a means to a career, there were certain boundaries that I could not cross. Science was science and religion was religion. Religious beliefs were exempt from objective scrutiny. They could not be challenged. The validity of belief was not up for discussion, it was sacrosanct. They had absorbed the truth of their beliefs from their parents or the Imams at the Madrassas (schools for teaching the Qur'ân) that some of them had attended when younger, after a day's normal schooling. They had been indoctrinated to the extent that not even an earthquake was likely to induce any change of mind. It is perhaps instructive that I use the word "indoctrinated". I have no difficulty in recognising this process in the religious practices of others. Yet I would never have used such a term to describe the source of my own religious convictions.

When I was young, I often heard two particular arguments advanced to try and bolster the claim that "*Christianity must be the truth.*" The arguments rested upon the facts that Christianity not only survived from the most difficult and unpromising of beginnings, but also that it went on to conquer the entire Roman Empire without the use of force. Surely, only a movement that God was behind could achieve what Christianity had achieved? Second was the testimony of all the martyrs. Surely there could not be so many people willing to die for something that was not true?

Today, however, these arguments pose a great problem: if survival and growth, or willingness to suffer martyrdom, are guarantees of authenticity, then Islam has as great a claim to authenticity as has Christianity, even if force was used as a primary means of spreading the religion in its earliest days. And whether a person of religious persuasion is a Christian, or a Muslim, or indeed anything else is more an accident of birth than any choice. That being the case, the whole of Christian belief in salvation and eternal life is largely dependent on chance. This is hardly a satisfactory system or even a believable system for any God to have come up with.

Experience tells us that very few people ever change their religious beliefs once they are set. We know that the number of converts from any one of the three monotheistic religions to any other of them is, to put it bluntly, negligible. Many may lapse into a dormant religious belief in later life, or reach a position when religion is just not important to them, but there are very few that convert from one faith to another as a result of intellectual conviction. Rather, most "conversions" in times past have been for pragmatic reasons or the result of coercion, often following conquest. The genuineness of all such conversions must raise considerable suspicion.

This should not surprise us. As already mentioned, physicist and Nobel Prize winner Max Planck observed that human beings find it extraordinarily difficult to change their minds and accept new truth, and the older people become the harder change becomes. And if that is the case, then Christian belief forces us to conclude that God created human beings in such a way that he would never be able to reach the vast majority of them with any revelation of himself, unless he was willing to offer different revelations of himself to different groups of people.

This last idea finds expression in the comfortable notion that all religions eventually lead to God. However, any study of the three great monotheistic religions of Judaism, Christianity and Islam shows that they are simply not compatible with each other. These religions not only offer different ways to God, they all claim, implicitly or explicitly, to be the only way to God. Making a sensible, informed choice between them is virtually impossible since this would require a considerable knowledge of the Bible and the Qu'rân, to say nothing of all the other religions that exist. How many would have the time to acquire this knowledge in the modern world? Such concerns can, and are, washed away with a dismissive wave of the hand by evangelical Christians with the reassuring thought that "*nothing is impossible with God*" (Luke 1:37). Evangelical Christians are very good at dismissive hand-waving.

One famous story in the Old Testament (1 Kings 18:16-46) tells how the prophet Elijah solved one conflict between different religious beliefs by arranging a contest on Mount Carmel. Elijah's God won by producing a miracle of fire after Baal had failed to show up. What a pity that resolutions of such intractable problems cannot be achieved in the same way today. That, of course, is because nobody has sufficient faith in their God to believe that he would show up when needed. Indeed, they know that he would not.

The obvious conclusion to this, however, is never drawn. Nobody is prepared to admit that their beliefs have no basis in reality. Why do we find it so easy to believe in miracles that happened long ago and far away? Why do so many refuse to accept the more likely explanation that the contest on Mount Carmel was a very convenient, entertaining but fabricated story told to bolster belief in the God of the Israelites?

The unfortunate truth is that there is no way to prove the claims of one religion over that of another. If it was possible, we would have found a way to demonstrate it by now. If any God existed, surely he would be willing to validate his own claims as opposed to the claims of some other, rival God? There are Christian evangelists who claim that they have openly challenged Muslims to see if their God can do the same miracles that the Christian God can do. Such "miracles", though claimed, never seem possible to verify. Why did Jesus apparently validate his own claims through precisely this vehicle (Luke 7:22), but now seems unwilling to empower his followers to validate the claims that they make on his behalf by the same methods?

Chapter 16   SCIENCE AND RELIGION

It was near the end of my teaching career that I ran the course on Science and Religion for sixth form students. Initially, I began with the idea that there was not necessarily a clash between the two because they could be said to deal with different aspects of reality. Science was to do with the study of cause and effect and discovering the laws and relationships that appear to govern the workings of the Universe and everything in it. Religion was to do with the ultimate question of the meaning of life: what are we doing here and what is the purpose (if any) of our being here? Hence there did not appear to be any necessary overlap and therefore no grounds for incompatibility. Stephen Jay Gould, the eminent Harvard biologist, refers to this idea as NOMA or Non-overlapping Magisteria. Perhaps, however, the reality is that I desperately wanted to believe that there was no overlap because I wanted Christianity to be "the truth" and was in no rush to find evidence that would in any way impinge on its credibility.

Nevertheless, as soon as I started to take a serious and careful look at these two realms of human activity, I began to realise that science and religion have completely different approaches to the way they operate, and in this they certainly are incompatible. Science attempts to find order from observations and measurements, to discover any underlying coherence in our everyday world, to find rational explanations for the things that happen. It may sometimes start with a preconceived idea or hypothesis, but it will always proceed to seek concrete evidence, some observations and preferably some measurements that will support or disprove the hypothesis. It requires any conclusions to be corroborated by evidence from other sources and spends considerable amounts of time trying to disprove its own hypotheses.

Religion, on the other hand, starts with a supposition that there is a God and that this God has made known his will regarding how human beings should relate to him and to each other. It depends upon the idea of revelation, which may occur as a series of one-off events, none of which can be tested or replicated, and these "revelations" eventually reach the status of something which cannot be challenged—an issue that is not open to discussion. You accept it by "faith" and you become governed by it. That is the starting point from which all else follows.

Hence, fundamentalist Jews, Christians or Muslims are not in the business of questioning their beliefs to make sure that they are compatible with the world in which they find themselves. Unlike scientists, they are not open to any new truth which is in conflict with old, revealed truth. Rather, the world and all the facts that may have been discovered about it are all required to fit in with the knowledge supposedly revealed to our distant ancestors. When this is not possible, knowledge gained from scientific observation and human reasoning power is always the casualty. For fundamentalist religious believers, the truth has already been revealed and it is complete and fixed. There is no room for any new ideas that might in any way conflict with past revelation. The more educated evangelicals may make room for some new understanding of revealed truth, but not where this involves faith and conduct or morals. Homosexuality lies within this realm.

The issue of homosexuality is so contentious precisely because it is here that the overlap is clear and the issue cannot be fudged. Homosexuality is usually thought of as a moral issue and morality is generally regarded as the province of religion. However, it is an area that also lends itself to objective scrutiny or scientific observation. Homosexuals can be interviewed, they can be subject to treatment in an attempt to change their sexual orientation (which means, when put in less euphemistic terms, that they can be experimented upon) or they can be prayed for in the hope of achieving a "cure". Vast amounts of information can be collected and analysed and conclusions can be drawn. A cure is something that can be subjected to verification, although this is by no means as easy as it sounds. Further studies on homosexuality in animals and birds can also be carried out.

All of these things, of course, have been done. Over many years, homosexuals were subject to some appalling treatments in the effort to affect a cure, most of which are no longer permitted in civilised society. The vast amount of data that has accrued from all this investigation has led an overwhelming majority of people from the scientific establishment to reject the religious opinion that seems to regard homosexuality as a sickness and homosexual activity as something that is immoral. The report on human sexuality by the Royal College of Psychiatrists (31 October 2007), makes the suggestion that homosexuals in stable relationships that are recognised by society are likely to have better physical and mental health.

Studies on animals and birds have revealed some specifically homosexual behaviour, a significant finding given that behaviour in all life forms other than human is assumed to be driven by instinct, without any element of moral choice. If some animals, acting naturally, exhibit homosexual behaviour, why should human beings be any different? And if something exists that we are unable to change then it is surely right to question whether we should feel entitled to prohibit behaviour that may result from it, as long as that behaviour cannot be clearly shown to be detrimental to the wellbeing of others. If there is any doubt at all, then should not homosexuals be entitled to the benefit of whatever doubt there may be? At the moment, that is clearly not the case in most religious communities.

It is commonly pointed out in Christian circles that not all of medical opinion is in agreement when it comes to the matter of homosexuality. There is some truth in this. However, the vast majority of these dissenting professionals are religious believers whose religion denounces homosexuality. Consequently, they are not in a good position to make objective judgements. Opinions that may have been influenced by preconceived ideas do not qualify as "scientific". Science consists of the formulation of agreed conclusions based on observations and/or measurements that can be repeated by others. Religious beliefs, which are not shared by everybody and cannot be substantiated, cannot be stirred into the mix if the conclusions are to lay claim to scientific status and have any credibility.

The specifically religious professional bodies that represent the psychiatrists and psychologists who regard homosexuality as a treatable condition are very small in comparison with the other, non-religious professional bodies, which hold the opposing view. Furthermore, there are many religious individuals in the latter group. It is the minority opinion only to which evangelical Christians turn when seeking respectability for their views.

Chapter 17   PAPAL INFALLIBILITY

The doctrine of Papal infallibility was formally declared in 1870 by Pope Pius IX. This, almost certainly, made official something that was already taken for granted. Whatever is the precise meaning of the doctrine is immaterial. It clearly implies that any official pronouncement made by the Pope, speaking on behalf of the Catholic Church, can be considered to have divine authority behind it. To put it another way, the Pope would be speaking on behalf of God. There is nothing sensational about this – the Church had for centuries believed that it was God's instrument for conveying his truth and implementing his will on the Earth.

When this doctrine is put into practice, however, there can be unfortunate consequences. The Church, clearly, has not always spoken for God, a fact which has finally been acknowledged. One who was to fall victim to the Church's idea of its own position in the world was the Italian mathematician, physicist and astronomer, Galileo Galilei. In the early seventeenth century, Galileo went public in his support of the Copernican model of the Solar System. In this model, the Sun was at the centre and the planets, including the Earth, were in orbit around it.

The prevailing model at the time, adhered to by the Church and supported by a literalist interpretation of the Bible, was one with a stationary Earth at the centre. Joshua told the Sun (and Moon) to stand still because he assumed that the Sun orbited the Earth (Joshua 10:13). He did not tell the Earth to stand still (or to stop rotating on its axis, which is what really needed to happen). Things came to a head in 1632, when Galileo was hauled before the Inquisition on charges of believing and teaching ideas not supported by the Church. He was essentially convicted of heresy, forced to recant, and was then placed under house arrest for the last ten years of his life.

This was an important episode in history. It shows the Church as a reactionary body that opposed what eventually turned out to be new truth. Today, everybody knows that Galileo was right, but we tend to forget that this is only because it is what we have been told. We implicitly rely on the credibility of the people who tell us these things. There is no simple demonstration that can be performed to verify the fact. The knowledge and mathematical reasoning needed to come to this conclusion are not straightforward; they were certainly not straightforward in Galileo's time. It is possible that none of the people immediately connected with the trial would have been capable of understanding all of Galileo's arguments. What was really at stake was the matter of Church authority: where was the ultimate source of truth to be found and whose prerogative was it to decide what this truth was?

The consequence of this clash between Galileo and the Church was that meaningful science disappeared from Italy for a very considerable period. Fortunately for the rest of us, the Reformation had restricted the power of the Catholic Church and science was able to progress in England and parts of Europe where the advent of Protestantism made these places more amenable to new ideas, especially, no doubt, if the Catholic Church was seen to oppose them.

The Catholic Church clearly could not have been representing the mind of God in 1632 and there is no reason to suppose that it does so now. The present Pope, Benedict XVI, has made his own view on homosexuality, and hence the official position of the Catholic Church, very clear: it is a practice that is condemned. However, it is pertinent to ask whether Pope Benedict XVI is likely to know anything more about human sexuality in 2011 than Pope Urban VIII knew about astronomy in 1632. The quality of life for large numbers of people the world over depends upon the answer to this question. Sadly, if the Pope's opinions are based on nothing more than his reading of the Bible, the answer to that question will be "*He does not.*"

As a postscript to all this, the Catholic Church officially reconsidered its position on astronomy in 1992 and in 2000 issued a general apology to those it now considered it had treated wrongly in the past, including Galileo. Ironically, the Vatican now has its own astronomical observatories.

Chapter 18 UNDESIRABLE CONSEQUENCES

Italian science may have been the loser in the battle between Galileo's science and the Catholic Church's beliefs, but Britain has not been immune from the consequences that can follow from religious belief. In 1952, mathematician and computer scientist Alan Turing was arrested and convicted of a homosexual act. Homosexuality was still a criminal offence at that time, but this law was a reflection of the beliefs of a society that regarded itself as being predominantly Christian.

Homosexuality was looked upon as an affliction and was presumed to be treatable. Turing was apparently offered a choice: accept hormone treatment (chemical castration) or go to prison. He chose the former, but sadly the side-effects were little short of horrendous and he was found dead from cyanide poisoning in 1954 when he was still only 41. Whether this was suicide or an accident will never be known but the underlying cause was, without question, his homosexuality and the Church-driven attitude of society towards this at the time.

Alan Turing was a long-distance runner, reputedly of Olympic standard, who may have represented his country in the 1948 Olympics had he not sustained an unfortunate injury. He was one of the most brilliant mathematicians of his age and his influence on the development of computers was immense. He was responsible for the design and construction of a decoding machine while working at Bletchley Park, the British centre for code-breaking operations, during the Second World War. There are many who believe that his contribution to the successful outcome of the war is impossible to overestimate.

There was every reason for the nation to be very grateful, but sadly, gratitude was in short supply for several outstanding members of the Bletchley Park decoding team once their immediate usefulness was deemed to be over, and it was non-existent for Alan Turing when his homosexuality became public knowledge. One certain consequence of his treatment and his untimely and needless death was that Britain lost one of its most able minds, something that did not help the British cause in the fledgling field of computer technology. There can be real consequences for human beings and even nations when policy is based on ideas that are unsupported by anything other than religious conviction.

By all accounts, Alan Turing was a shy, pleasant and inoffensive human being. He certainly had outstanding talent and stands as an example of the huge contribution that a homosexual can make to society when they are given the opportunity to do so. Tragically, his many fine qualities were to count for nothing in the end. He was to be judged on one attribute, whose importance was deemed to be sufficient to outweigh all other considerations, and by people with considerably less intellectual capability than Alan Turing. There was never any evidence to show that anybody else might be inconvenienced or suffer any adverse consequences from what he was doing, except that it was assumed that it would offend the sensibilities of most people in a supposedly Christian nation.

In September 2009, Gordon Brown, the British Prime Minister at the time, made a public apology for the way that Alan Turing had been treated fifty-seven years earlier. Although this was of little use to Alan Turing himself, the apology was important because it does show that, outside of Church circles, official attitudes and opinions have changed for the better in the intervening years, as society continues to move slowly out of the dark ages towards a little more enlightenment.

As I write this, one of today's newspapers carried a report of the sentencing of three young people for a vicious, unprovoked attack on a 62 year old gay civil servant in Trafalgar Square. Mr Baynham, who died as a result of the injuries that he sustained, was deliberately targeted because of his presumed homosexuality according to the report. He may not have been a Galileo or an Alan Turing, but he was a human being who did not deserve to die in the way that he did. The attack, apparently, was fuelled by alcohol. But whereas alcohol may fuel anger, it does not make a person homophobic. What does encourage homophobia and lend some justification in the eyes of the perpetrators for their actions, is when highly respected institutions, supposed guardians of the nation's morality, continue to condemn homosexual practice. *"If the Church can condemn it, why can't I?"* Homophobic murders may be much more rare in this country than they are in the USA, but when they are quite unnecessary, one is one too many.

In the summer of 2008, the prominent Northern Ireland politician, Iris Robinson, was reported to have made some exceedingly homophobic comments. Again, there is only one reason that any prominent person would ever do this and it is because they feel that their views are respectable because they are supported by an organisation, one of whose principal functions is to set the moral tone for society. The Church is seen as the upholder of all that is good. Rarely are its views in these areas publicly challenged. Any organisation that wishes to discriminate against a particular group of people should at least be held accountable and the Church should be no exception.

Chapter 19   DANGERS OF FUNDAMENTALISM

It was once assumed (and may still be assumed) by the liberal, chattering classes in Britain that reason and common sense will lead most religious people, over time, to adopt "moderate" views. This implies views that are informed by reason and are capable of accommodating differing opinions. There is some truth, however, in the assertion that people who hold moderate views are often lacking in conviction. Fundamentalism, of course, is all about conviction and certainty. It is about the most intensely held beliefs, beliefs that are so strong that people may be willing to die or to kill for them.

Anyone who is familiar with modern trends in religion would have every reason to doubt such complacent assumptions of our liberal democracy. Evangelical Anglican colleges are over-subscribed while liberal colleges struggle for students. Fundamentalist Christian churches are increasing in both numbers and membership, much of it driven by Christian television channels which saturate the airwaves with their message in almost every country in the world. The really large churches are generally fundamentalist in outlook. The membership is committed. Religion is their life, not some pastime. It produces such passion because it relies heavily on personal experience, and there is no doubt that there is a life-transforming power somewhere in all this.

These are the churches where you will find reformed alcoholics, drug addicts, prostitutes, thieves, indeed reformed ne'er do wells of every kind. All of this because they "met" with Jesus; they invited him into their lives, became "born again", received a fresh start and were infused with the power to change. And change they have. If that is your experience, you are likely to be enthusiastic about it, full of conviction and evangelistic zeal. Fundamentalist churches are made up of such people.

All of this is to be lauded and it is impossible to argue with the "success" that it visibly produces. It is based on a very powerful message—the fact that through one man's death, forgiveness and a fresh start with divine help becomes possible. I know all this because I have been a member of more than one such church and know of other similar churches. But none of this provides irrefutable evidence of the other central tenet of their beliefs—that the Bible is the truth in its totality. This belief, coupled with the view not infrequently held by fundamentalists of Christian or Islamic persuasion that they are doing God a great favour if they manage to impose their views on society in general, is where the danger lies. Fundamentalism is characterised by fanaticism and intolerance – and religion is characterised by a tendency to gravitate towards fundamentalism.

The danger of living in a society where this kind of idea gains the ascendency becomes obvious when we look at the past. All three of the monotheistic religions have, or have had, laws of heresy (wrong belief or belief that is not sanctioned by the religious authorities whose opinions hold sway in that particular religion) and blasphemy (unacceptable utterances, as defined by the religion, relating to God or even one of his prophets, including the claim to be in any way equal with God). Freedom of thought in societies that have been dominated by religious belief was generally discouraged but more often suppressed outright.

While in Peru, I had the chance to visit the Palace of the Inquisition in the centre of the capital, Lima. It is the place where the Inquisition once inflicted the most horrendous tortures on its hapless victims. It is now a museum and preserves many of the instruments of torture exactly as they must have been 1821 when Spanish rule in Peru, along with the Inquisition, came to an end and the dungeons below ground were sealed off. They were rediscovered by accident early in the twentieth century during restoration work. The Inquisition was an arm of the Catholic Church for several hundred years, being used, amongst other things, to enforce uniformity of belief. My visit to these dungeons was an extremely chilling experience. Who knows what it must have been like for the prisoners who were taken down there to experience justice at the hands of God's servants?

Many fundamentalist Christians in the USA would ban the teaching of evolution in schools in favour of the Bible's creation story. They would not even allow the two to be taught side by side. Even in churches in Britain, I have heard many preachers deride Darwin and evolution, and proclaim that there is not a shred of evidence to support what they imagine to be his idea. If you were to ask any of these preachers just how many pages of Darwin's book they had read, the honest answer would be, in almost every case, "*None.*" Anybody who has read Darwin's book, which is not always easy to understand if you happen to be unfamiliar with some of the biological terms, cannot but be impressed with Darwin's almost encyclopaedic knowledge of his subject. His conviction that the facts, even as known in those days, pointed to the inescapable conclusion that the process of evolution by natural selection was by far the most viable explanation on offer, becomes somewhat difficult for a thinking person to refute.

Admittedly, Darwin never claimed that the arguments were conclusive without any shadow of doubt. He was well aware of the difficulties in his theory. In other words, he was well versed in the arguments on the other side. What a contrast to the average evangelical Christian who, often totally ignorant of the facts on the scientific side, proceeds to insist on his own explanation of creation by God in the Garden of Eden, without, apparently, the need for any evidence to support it.

The truth regarding this conflict is the complete opposite of what so many fundamentalist Christian preachers confidently assert. It is the fundamentalist preachers who have no hard evidence for their beliefs. Darwin, in contrast, had a great deal of carefully sifted evidence, and was confident that time would provide the necessary facts to fill the gaps and overcome all the objections to his (and Alfred Russell Wallace's) theory. Since Darwin published his book, time has seen huge developments in the biological sciences, from Mendel's laws of inheritance to the discovery of chromosomes and the unravelling of the structure of DNA and now to the modern science of genetics. A lot of the knowledge gained has helped towards understanding how the mechanisms of natural selection work. What none of this knowledge has done so far is to refute Darwin's ideas or offer any support whatsoever for the belief in creationism.

The most disconcerting fact about all of this is that such fundamentalist views seem to go unchallenged by members of the congregation, even the university educated ones. And if you do get the chance to speak to any of the preachers, which is not very often, you are likely to be told "*Look, brother (or sister), you have to make up your mind. Do you want to believe God's word or do you want to believe the opinions of these so-called scientists?*" Thus, all discussion is stifled. In fact, I never found any forum in any Church over a forty year period where any of the dubious ideas that were presented as fact could be challenged or where honest doubts could be expressed, and certainly no forum where they could be discussed.

Interestingly, Darwin's theory has a parallel in the physical sciences. The principle (or law as it is more commonly referred to) of the conservation of energy is a fundamental idea, one of the bedrocks of the physical sciences upon which much else rests. It cannot be proved to be true, but nobody seems anxious to reject it on this basis. If it was not true then it should be possible to demonstrate that it is false. We are entitled to place our confidence in it as long as nobody is able to do this. It is exactly the same with evolution.

Darwin's ideas provide the basis upon which much of biology rests and upon which much of our present understanding of life has been built. In a society dominated by fundamentalists, all such progress would be put in jeopardy. The effects of fundamentalism on society and scientific progress have indeed already been witnessed. In both China and Russia, some scientific endeavours are known to have proceeded down blind alleys by being made to conform to political ideologies, which are themselves just another form of fundamentalism of a type often practised by totalitarian regimes.

In Britain today, there is already much debate about the morality of stem cell research and the use of genetically modified crops to name just two important issues. No-one would pretend that all such matters are easy to resolve. We may never know whether it is "moral" or not to pursue stem cell research, assuming that moral has some objective meaning. What we do know for certain is that such research offers the possibility of great benefits in the future, and we are even now watching many benefits inch closer towards reality. Yet if many religious people, speaking from the higher moral plane of their religious convictions, had been allowed to have their way, none of this would have happened.

Can the human race be blamed if God has entrusted to us more knowledge than we are able to handle? Should we abandon our search for greater understanding and knowledge on the grounds that some of our quest may be offensive to our Creator? If there was a God who is so concerned about his laws and values being adhered to, then we have to ask why he has so far done nothing in the face of all the abortions that have taken place in the clinics of the western world for over forty years.

Those who do not recognise the immense power of fundamentalism in the Christian Church should take a look at religious broadcasting. Fundamentalist Christian groups own the vast majority of Christian television broadcasting stations. The effect of this is already noticeable not only in England and the USA but also many developing countries. The fundamentalists realised at an early stage that the most effective way to spread any message was by means of television broadcasting. The dawning of the satellite era made it possible to reach regions of the world that traditional methods could never reach. They have not been mistaken. Countless millions of dollars of investment have provided them with an unparalleled platform from which to spread their brand of the Gospel to the four corners of the Earth.

Although I would never refer to evangelical (or fundamentalist) Christianity as a sect on account of the fact that it is far too widespread for that term to describe it accurately, it nevertheless shares a number of features that typically characterise a sect. One of these characteristics is to try and impose a rigorous doctrinal viewpoint and discourage any open debate that might question the assumptions made.

I remember being in a young people's fellowship meeting in Uganda, many years ago. There were only about a dozen of us, aged between 15 and 25, and so the atmosphere was more informal than usual. It was certainly informal enough for one young girl to admit that she never felt able to share her real concerns in fellowship meetings because she felt that only certain contributions were welcome.

Welcome contributions were anything regarding your victories in life and how God had blessed you; unwelcome ones were those which expressed doubts and admitted to difficulties because these things were seen as not being conducive to building up the faith of the brothers and sisters. Consequently, real issues were not dealt with, resulting in people not quite living in the world as it actually is. The use of "authority" to discourage or suppress genuine concerns can prevent people from forming honest and meaningful relationships and the consequences of this are often hidden behind an acceptable religious façade. This was demonstrated in another experience that I had whilst in Uganda.

There was an occasion when I attended a big Christian conference for young people in Mombasa, Kenya. I made the long journey from Nairobi with some friends and we arrived a little later than hoped, when the first evening meeting had already begun and a time of "free worship" was in progress. For those unfamiliar with this idea it is a time when everybody is encouraged to worship God "as the Spirit moves them." The general melee of noise that ensues from this means than no one will be able to pay attention to anything you may be doing and so there is a kind of freedom not normally encountered in more formal worship. People are often encouraged to "speak in tongues" at these times.

However, having arrived late and entered at the back, I was immediately struck by a particularly pretty African girl, or more properly young woman as she looked to be in her mid-twenties. She seemed to be somewhere in the heavens having some kind of ecstatic worship experience. I have to admit to a little jealousy. Whereas I enjoyed such times of free worship, I could not, at that time, ever remember entering a realm of such obvious blessing myself.

I did not notice her again during the conference. However, when I was travelling back home and had just crossed the border into Uganda, I decided to visit a Christian girl who was teaching at a school a short way from the border crossing. I was actually hoping for a cup of tea and any other refreshment that might be on offer in the hard times that Uganda was by then experiencing. Many cafés in the local towns that once might have offered refreshment had long since closed under Idi Amin's regime and the country's collapsed economy. Fortunately, she was at home and was with two or three other Christian teachers when I arrived. One of these was the young woman I had noticed at the conference. The subsequent conversation eventually got around to discussing the conference and this young woman then confided something quite astounding. She said: "*I am always disappointed at these conferences, because everybody else seems to 'get blessed' whereas I never feel anything.*"

Never feel anything? I had imagined her to be on cloud nine when I saw her. How we can be deceived by appearances. Not that this young woman had had any intention of trying to deceive anyone, she was simply trying to conform, doing what she had been encouraged to do in order to receive a blessing. Nobody was encouraged afterwards to make an honest assessment of the blessing that they felt they had actually received. Rather, there was group pressure to say what a wonderful meeting it had been, how there had been a mighty move of God in our midst, how anointed the preacher had been and so on and so forth. Her honesty at this moment led to an hour of real, meaningful fellowship even if it did raise some uncomfortable questions. It may have been a small incident, but it left a big and lasting impression on me.

And so much later, when it came to the critical issue of homosexuality that had intruded into my life, this lack of openness, lack of any real dialogue, endless reiteration of entrenched positions and the lack of reality began to have a corrosive effect. It was further exacerbated by what seemed a relentless move towards Bible literalism in the church that I attended. I found that there was a gulf beginning to open up, not just between myself and the Church but also between myself and Christian belief. I was driven to take a fresh look at the Bible, as far as that is possible. That is the subject of my next book.

Chapter 20   LAKEWOOD CHURCH

I include this section to show that I am aware of this church and of a number of similar, very successful churches. Members of these churches often assume that if the rest of us belonged to such churches, all our doubts would disappear. I have, over the years, belonged to some very successful churches and I was an ardent admirer of Joel Osteen, the senior pastor of Lakewood Church, and also of other very high profile ministers of the Gospel such as T.D. Jakes and Creflo Dollar. I watched their satellite television broadcasts for several years. Despite the undoubted success of these preachers and of their churches, however, I am now convinced that all of it is built on a premise that is, in fact, false.

Joel, in particular, represents the desirable face of the evangelical/charismatic world. He comes from a family with very impressive Christian credentials. Lakewood Church was founded by his father, John, in 1959. John had been a pastor with the Southern Baptist congregations but left after disagreements to found his own Church. The disagreements arose on account of John's experiences with one of his daughters, Lisa, who was born with some form of cerebral palsy. Doctors said that she was unlikely to enjoy any sort of normal life.

John and his wife, Dodie, were devastated by this news and he took time away from his pastoral responsibilities to pray and seek God. His searching of the Bible convinced him that God was a God of healing and not just a God of salvation. He and Dodie set about praying for their daughter's recovery and began to see some wonderful improvements in her health. He was encouraged to proclaim his new convictions to the congregation, but this did not meet with universal approval and he felt obliged to resign his position as pastor. He and about one hundred like-minded church members formed a new congregation in a disused building somewhere nearby.

John and Dodie Osteen apparently experienced many miraculous provisions from God during his lifetime. In 1981, after a protracted illness, Dodie was diagnosed with terminal metastatic cancer of the liver. Her deliverance from this death sentence is told in her inspiring booklet *Healed from Cancer*. When John died after forty successful years pastoring the Church at Lakewood, the congregation had grown to around 8,000.

John was succeeded by his younger son, Joel, who took over the responsibilities of Senior Pastor despite having no previous experience of any kind of public speaking and no formal training in the ministry. He quickly showed, however, that he had absorbed a great deal from the ministry and example of his father. So successful has he been that the Church soon outgrew its premises. Joel tells the story of how God's miraculous provision enabled them to acquire a football stadium in the centre of Houston and convert it into an auditorium with seating for 15,000. This auditorium is filled three times each Sunday and the number associated with the church was estimated to be approaching fifty thousand at the time that I stopped tuning in to the broadcasts, a reluctant decision born out of the desire to preserve our marriage.

Joel openly says that he has so much experience of God's faithfulness that it is too late to try and convince him that there is no God. I would not wish to try and do so. There are thousands of people who would no doubt testify to how their lives have been improved by following the principles advocated by Joel in his sermons and his books. Anyone who has experienced the things that Joel has experienced is entitled to have a strong, unshakeable faith. And his message is very attractive, positive and full of encouragement. He and his wife exude joy and certainty.

I wrote to Joel and sent him a copy of the book, *Prayers for Bobby*. I received no reply. Joel is a very busy man with a hugely successful local church and a worldwide television ministry. Homosexuality, no doubt, does not figure highly on his agenda because it is so obviously wrong. The Bible says it is and so, presumably, it needs no explanation or discussion.

For all his undoubted qualities, Joel has beliefs about the Bible that I find completely untenable. On his website, the beliefs upon which his ministry is based are stated, and the beliefs regarding the Bible are reiterated at the start of every service that he, or any of his pastors, presides over in the Church. The website statement reads: "*We believe the **entire** Bible is inspired by God, **without error** and the authority on which we base our faith, conduct and doctrine*" [emphasis added]. Although I cannot be absolutely certain, having followed his ministry for several years my suspicion is that he views the entire Bible as literal truth. A short version of the "confession" that he and the entire congregation, holding Bibles aloft, make at the start of every Church service is as follows: "*This is my Bible. I am what it says I am. I have what it says I have. I can do what it says I can do. Today I'll be taught the Word of God. I boldly confess, my mind is alert, my heart is receptive, I will never be the same. In Jesus' Name, Amen.*"

While I cannot deny the success of this ministry, I certainly cannot reconcile it with the fact that it is all based on a belief about the Bible that it is impossible to defend using any objective criteria. The evidence appears to be largely contained within the personal experiences of Joel's immediate family and members of his and possibly other churches.

Chapter 21   CONCLUDING THOUGHTS

The journey that I have made began with the search for a "cure" for my gay son. It subsequently transpired that there were no certifiable cases of anyone having managed to procure a long term change in their sexual orientation. Further, St. Paul's explanation of the cause of homosexuality in the book of Romans was clearly at odds with the fact that a significant number of evangelical Christian people, brought up in evangelical Christian families, have turned out to be homosexual. In this regard, there does not appear to be any obvious statistical difference that might differentiate between Christian and non-Christian families.

The end result of all this was that I came to accept that my son was gay, would always be gay, and almost certainly had always been gay. He never made a choice to be gay and there is nothing that either I or my wife could have done would that have produced a different outcome. We have both come to love him the way that he is, not the way that we might have wanted him to be. Our love is that of any parent and it is not conditional.

This knowledge places me in a position that is in sharp contrast to that of the Christian people amongst whom I spent most of my life. Sadly, in their eyes my son remains an abomination, or at least the lifestyle that he has "chosen" to follow is an abomination. This is because they base their beliefs on the teachings of a book that I am now certain contains nothing more than the beliefs and aspirations of an ancient people. The

Bible is not the Word of God that I had always assumed it to be and most Christians still believe it to be. This left my position as a Christian on the verge of becoming untenable, although even at this stage I was unwilling to admit to what was clearly staring me in the face.

My observations of, and dealings with, the Anglican Church, persuaded me that there is not a shred of evidence that would lead anyone to believe the claim that it is a Church "*led by the Holy Spirit.*" There is far more visible evidence to suggest that it consists of people who are at the mercy of public opinion, the approval of their peers or the beliefs they accepted long ago and which they never examined in any critical manner. Indeed, I would go further and say that there does not seem to be any difference between leaders within the Church and leaders in any other section of society. When their beliefs are questioned, they react in exactly the same way as that in which we might expect a politician to react: with evasion, hypocrisy, humbug and scarcely concealed hatred for those with an opposing viewpoint. This overall conclusion is not restricted to members of the Anglican Church. It is true of many people that I have come across in a number of different churches.

None of this, in itself, proved sufficient for me to give up on forty years of belief. What it did was to motivate me to search the Bible, to see for myself exactly what foundation my beliefs had been built on. What was believable? As it turned out, much less than I had previously imagined. The entire New Testament is riddled with anomalies and uncertainties and shows strong evidence that beliefs about Jesus grew over time. Major doctrines regarding the person of Jesus find little unequivocal support when we look at the Bible narratives taken together. Of course, they never were looked at together when Christian belief was being formed.

I harbour the hope that any Christian who has managed to read this far will be sufficiently intrigued to read the sequel to this story. Originally written as part of this book, the difference in style (there is more factual argument and less personal emphasis) and the amount of material involved dictated that it would be better published as a separate book. Although I would like to call it an academic study, it is not "serious scholarship" in the sense that it does not need any special knowledge or anything beyond normal intelligence to follow the arguments. They are based on the most obvious interpretation of the English texts.

However, they do raise serious questions of a fundamental nature, questions that never surface in the circle of believers because leaders of all persuasions prefer them to be swept under the carpet. The issues must have been raised in academic circles, presumably many times, but there they appear to remain. They never seem to percolate down to the ordinary believer, probably because such ideas would be too unsettling and far too dangerous and vested interests make certain that the faithful are never troubled by such matters. Nobody wishes to risk rocking the boat. Religion, it seems, does not require people to have intellectual integrity, just something called faith mixed with emotion and loyalty.

I am all in favour of passion in religion. An encounter with a God of love cannot be an emotionally cold affair; it must be an all-consuming experience.

This is one of several reasons that attracted me to the Pentecostal and charismatic movements. I spent most of my life in such circles, although I never subscribed to their fundamentalist views—I was always more of a traditional evangelical in that regard.

However, I could not exist off a diet of unquestioning belief ("faith") and emotion alone. I needed something else besides, some sort of reliable foundation that stood apart from my personal experience. It is this "something else" that, in the end, turned out to be missing. It is why I must now classify myself as a very reluctant atheist, but an atheist nonetheless. Personal experience is not a reliable guide on its own and Christianity is not backed by sufficiently coherent evidence to make it credible. Christian beliefs are not Bible based, as is usually supposed but are rather based on what we choose to believe from the Bible's various, different accounts.

Chapter 22   MY WIFE'S STORY

I am contributing this as the result of the gentle but persistent encouragement from a lesbian friend. She is aware that my husband has written his book and she has read the manuscript. She says that it shows considerable insight into homosexuality but stressed that some input from me would be an invaluable addition. I have not read the book. I cannot bear to relive the past for it is still full of the most unbearable pain and heartache. Writing this little piece has been a trial, but I hope it will help to provide what will perhaps be a more complete picture and that it will be of benefit to somebody.

I am Peruvian and I grew up in a country with a very macho culture, where gay men are openly mocked and insulted; where to have a gay child is an embarrassment and a shame for any family and a thing to be kept secret at all costs. Homosexuality is considered something weird, perverted and against nature—God only created heterosexual men and women, not any other category of people. My own feelings were a little different. I was always sorry for the men that I saw in the streets who were obviously gay and I even tried to be friendly towards some of them. However, I was never able to comprehend how they had come to be the way they were.

When my son was young, I was aware that some of his mannerisms, some of his very expressive gestures, reminded me of young gay men that I had known in my country, and it frightened me. The feelings dissipated somewhat when he reached his teenage years and he made friends with two or three girls, although none of these ever reached the status of girlfriend as I had hoped. However, there was a boy who was quite a close friend, who admitted to being gay when he was sixteen years old. I remember my son being visibly upset by this and he assured me that he was not gay himself. Nevertheless, the revelation was a cause for more anxiety and I did whatever I could to discourage the friendship, fearful that it might influence my own boy to go down the same path. Maybe I was even afraid that homosexuality was in some way contagious.

Around this time, a Latin American friend confided in me that huge problems had arisen in her family because a cousin of hers appeared to be on the edge of a nervous breakdown, brought on by the discovery that one of her sons was gay. Feelings of panic swept over me, a great knot forming in the pit of my stomach. I had an awful premonition that this could happen to me and I prayed fervently that it would not be so. I desperately hoped that while he was at university my son would find an environment where he could feel more at home and where he might find some girl that would be right for him.

I have vivid recollections of Boxing Day, 2005. When my son announced that he had something important to tell us, my heart leapt a little. The fleeting thought crossed my mind that he was perhaps about to tell us he had a girlfriend, that she was pregnant and that he was going to marry her. I would have jumped for joy if this had indeed been the case. Such illusions lasted but a moment, to be replaced at once, as I heard his actual words, with an indescribable sensation of fear, despair and panic, feelings that were awful beyond imagination.

Blinded by tears, I looked at my son but he had disappeared and I saw only a stranger. The days that followed were one continuous nightmare and I would wake up at night and sometimes go walking round the house, inwardly screaming in terror, unable to accept that any of this really was happening to me. There was an awful black shadow that had descended and now hovered over my life and it would not go away. I would go to my son's bedroom, hug his clothes and weep bitter tears for all that I had lost, weep for my precious boy.

I remember going on a shopping trip with a Christian friend, someone that I felt I could trust and confide in. She detected that there was something wrong and asked me what the matter was. When I broke down crying and told her about my son, her reply was that we must pray for his healing. I was grateful for her concern and her reassurance that everything would be alright, that God was greater that the devil. But once I was alone again, I was desolate.

Sometime in early January, shortly after my son had come out to us, my elder son came to visit me, wanting to know how I was, not in his normal, casual way but clearly because he was concerned about my feelings regarding his younger brother. I could not hold back the tears and sobbed uncontrollably in his arms, spilling out all the anguish that had flooded my soul, wanting to know what I had done wrong. My elder son was, by now, six months away from completing a medical degree and was far more informed about these matters than either myself or my husband. He held me tight and said that it had nothing to do with the way we had brought up his brother, his brother had been born the way he was and nothing could have been done to change him.

He was well aware of the beliefs we held, but he had abandoned them a long time ago. He had some harsh words to say about those "*well-heeled, ignorant bigots*" as he referred to the TV evangelists, and he advised me to take no notice of what they said. In fact, even better, I should stop listening to them altogether. I did not follow his advice immediately, but as I continued to hear the hurtful things they said about homosexuals I did eventually stop listening to their broadcasts and began to resent the fact that my husband continued to do so.

My daughter also paid us an unexpected visit and I suspected that she had been in contact with her older brother and realised that I was not coping very well. Amidst copious tears, I confided to her my dreams, dreams of his being married and having children, dreams of his being happy in a way that meant something to me, dreams that were now in ruins. She let me finish and then said gently that these dreams were my dreams, they were not her younger brother's dreams. I had lived out my dreams up to the present and now I had to let her brother live out his dreams and find his own happiness in his own way. His dreams, whatever they were, were every bit as valid as any dreams that I might have had, and no matter what, he was still my son and her younger brother. We should not let anything come between us and that fact. She had grown up with the advantage of living in a more accepting country and belonging to a more accepting generation than my own.

Despite this advice, I was becoming very depressed and eventually went home to my country for a holiday. When I returned, feeling a lot better for having confided in my immediate family and found them to be more accepting, if not more understanding, than I feared might have been the case, I found my husband to be very changed. He was now obsessed with listening to Christian television broadcasts, convinced that God would heal our son. Suddenly, he had become almost impossible to talk to. It was as if we had become total strangers and I had lost my husband to a religious fanaticism. I felt abandoned and lonelier than ever and I began to spiral back into depression.

Attendance at church became an ordeal. I was now very isolated and lonely, no longer able to relate to anybody as I had done previously. The pastor of the church projected a very macho image in his ministry and could be very insensitive in the way that he expressed himself. I became more and more alienated. In desperation, we agreed to seek counselling for our deteriorating marriage, from a couple within the church. They were slightly older than we were and had been offering this free counselling service for a long time.

We chose to be as open as possible and told them about the problem with our son and the effect this was having on us. Unfortunately, they were out of their depth with this particular issue, and I cannot remember much of what they said except to tell us that they could not condone the lifestyle that our son had chosen to pursue.

This was more devastation and I was beginning to find more support and understanding from people outside the church than inside it. I was in turmoil, no longer sure what to pray for, and shortly afterwards I decided to sever all of my connections with the church.

Over a period of time I came to accept what my elder son and my daughter had told me: that my younger son had not chosen to express his sexuality in one particular way as opposed to some other way. He had never had any choice and he was simply expressing what he was, what he had always been. I no longer felt that he was someone in need of healing and I began to pray for his happiness instead.

Sometime later, he told us that he had a boyfriend. Deep down, I was shocked by this further revelation. My prayers appeared to have been answered but clearly I was not prepared for what this might mean. The reality of a boyfriend was a further step in the process of coming to terms with everything that homosexuality could involve, but I did not find it an easy step to take. However, I did notice that he seemed happier and more open. Perhaps it was me who had changed and possibly for that reason I felt more at ease in conversation with him.

I genuinely liked this boyfriend when we finally met him, and was deeply saddened when the relationship ended after a few years. My one desire for our son is that he will find happiness, somewhere, somehow. However, I know that I will have to learn to accept that he must find his own happiness in his own way and that I cannot help. Coming to terms with that fact when I am his mother has been another difficult step in this long journey. However, I find comfort in the fact that I now know God loves him as much as he loves me or anybody else. He is not a reject.

Very fortunately, my husband had some sort of conversion himself before we reached the divorce courts. Something that he had heard on a Christian television broadcast caused him to draw back and reconnect with the normal world. He lost his certainty and started to communicate in a way that I could understand once more. Slowly, we have been able to rebuild our marriage. I cannot pretend that things will ever be quite the same again, but at least we are together; we are comfortable once more in each other's company and we have found some new, shared happiness from the ashes of our original life. Both of us have come to a full acceptance of the fact that our son is gay. I love him now just as much as if he had been heterosexual. I just regret the long, wasted years when I feel that we lost some of our communication with him, years that can never be reclaimed.

My biggest regret in all of this is that I was brainwashed into accepting homophobic ideas both by the society that I grew up in and later by the constant barrage of homophobic comments from preachers who visited our church and the Christian broadcasts on satellite television. It causes me anguish that such views are still freely expressed in religious circles, continuing to foster prejudice against homosexuals and increasing the many difficulties they already face.

I can no longer subscribe to the ideas about God that I once held. My God offers his love to everybody who wishes to receive it. To accept this truth, to be able to escape from the bigotry of fanatical Christianity, has been a great release. It would be nice if young people growing up today could be actively encouraged to have more understanding and more tolerance so that nobody in future generations will have to face the unnecessary trauma that I (and no doubt my son) have had to cope with.

Chapter 23   OUR SON'S STORY

When my dad first told me that he was going to write a book about his experiences, I felt the same discomfort I think most people would feel if they knew that a parent was writing a book which might include uncomfortable disclosures about their offspring's teenage years. But it was clear that it was really important to him, so I agreed to contribute a chapter about my experiences in the hope that it would help to give him some closure, and possibly be of help to other people who might find themselves in a similar situation.

Looking back to my childhood, it's clear that I've always been gay, even though as a child I didn't know about such concepts. Despite the fact I tended to prefer toys and cartoons that were aimed at boys, the signs were always there, and I'm sure that any adult who was aware of homosexuality would have had their suspicions about me. It is obviously harder to accept things about which you have a lot prejudice and particularly if it happens to concern one of your own children.

I'd always been raised to believe I'd have girlfriends, get married, and have children. My parents were socially conservative Christians, so family values were high on the agenda, whereas candid discussion about modern issues was not. So initially, I thought I fancied girls and had a few false crushes. I didn't really fancy them, of course; they were just nice girls who I could tell were pretty. But fancying girls is what boys did, and I didn't have any other frame of reference at the time.

I didn't really know about homosexuality growing up. I'd had a sheltered Christian upbringing, and it's not the sort of thing I'd talk about with friends. Furthermore, under Section 28 (a piece of legislation which forbade the "promotion of homosexuality" in schools), it was even a taboo topic at school. The only time I'd hear the word "gay" was as a playground insult, so even before I knew what it meant, I inferred from the context it was used in that it must be something bad.

Therefore, it understandably caused me concern when I started to be attracted to other boys at the onset of puberty. Being gay was a really bad thing in my mind, so the feelings I was having made me feel worried and confused. Unable to accept it, I dismissed, suppressed, or ignored all the evidence—it must just be teenage hormones and confusion, and everything would sort itself out as I got older and had more experience with girls. It was textbook denial, but I wasn't in an environment where I could talk to anybody about it, or explore my feelings without fear of repercussions.

By the time I started sixth form, it seemed like everybody who was anybody would pull at parties and they started getting boyfriends and girlfriends, something which only exacerbated my situation, since I wasn't doing either of these things. Towards the end of lower sixth, one of my close friends told me that he was gay, and, even though I didn't have a problem with homosexuality on religious grounds in the same way my parents did, I remember my stomach knotted as if he'd just told me some awful news.

I spoke to a mutual female friend of ours that night about my concerns: he wouldn't be able to get married and have kids; he might get HIV; what if he fancied me? Wouldn't it make our friendship weird? My questions reflected just how little I knew about gay people. Fortunately, she allayed my fears and told me, sympathetically but frankly, that he was the same person he always was and I was being ridiculous. Although things were a little awkward at first, our friendship soon returned to normal.

The ironic thing is that I really shouldn't have been surprised by my friend's coming out. With hindsight, it really was quite obvious. But this demonstrates the capacity people can have for self-deception. If you believe something is bad, then you don't want to believe it either about yourself or about somebody close to you, even if it is something that is obvious to everybody else. It's often easier to make rationalizations than it is to face an unpalatable prospect. So, in that sense, I can understand how my parents must have felt about me.

It helped to see that our other mutual friends did not seem to be unduly perturbed on account of his being gay, although it was kept a closely guarded secret within our circle—homophobia was prevalent at my school and life would have been very difficult for anybody who was openly gay. It caused my own attitudes towards homosexuality to soften, and I was now completely fine with other people being gay. Yet, paradoxically, I still found it difficult to accept it in myself: I'd had it drilled into me from an early age that the only way to be truly happy in life was to get married and have children, and that's what I had my heart set on.

As sixth form continued, I felt increasingly isolated: I didn't really fit in with the guys, but I didn't fit in with the girls either. I was in an awkward hinterland at an age when I was desperate to belong. I became privately unhappy, and I didn't feel at ease in my social circle. Looking back, I can see it's because I wasn't being true to myself, and it's difficult to form proper friendships, let alone relationships, until you're comfortable with who you are.

When my brother and sister both left for university, my mother struggled to adjust to the emptiness of the house, and there was a surge in my parents' religious fervour. Televangelists from the USA, with their attendant anti-gay demagoguery, became a fixture on the TV. Despite my religious upbringing, my own religious beliefs had waned, and the fact that my parents followed teachings which I often found to be abhorrent made it increasingly difficult for me, as an adult, to relate to them.

It wasn't until I started university that I realised, slowly but with growing certainty, that the jig was up: I was gay, I always had been gay and I always would be gay, no matter how much I tried to change. It was scary because it would completely change the trajectory of my future from everything I'd always imagined it would be; at the same time, I finally had a clear sense of conviction about who I was, something that previously had always been lacking. It was finally time to deal with the issue; the only question was how best to do that.

I knew that my parents disapproved of homosexuality. At one point, my mum stopped watching a TV show because it had showed a lesbian kiss. They had obviously been uncomfortable about my having a gay friend when I was in sixth form as well. I realised that, while my gay friend's parents had been supportive (his mother had suspected he was gay from an early age and made it clear that she would love him no matter what), it was going to be a very different story with my own parents.

Unfortunately, as a student I was still somewhat dependent on my parents and coming out would have made the situation at home untenable. Knowing how religious they were, I suspected that they would be constantly praying for me, or having their church friends round trying to "heal" me or convert me. And that was the best case scenario. We were going to need time and space apart while they came to terms with it, and we wouldn't have that until I had flown the nest.

Not being able to come out to everybody meant I had the choice coming out to some people but not others (and all the difficulties that entails), or not coming out at all. Furthermore, until I had come out properly, I couldn't act upon my sexuality without leading some kind of furtive double life. Not wanting to do that, I decided to focus on other things until I had graduated and had a job, and was in a position to tell everybody myself, on my own terms, and in my own time.

Even though my being gay was the elephant in the room, I was still worried how my friends would react when I told them. What if they were upset that I hadn't told them sooner, or they somehow disapproved? People say that if your friends don't accept you for who you are, they aren't really your friends anyway, but such platitudes aren't very comforting when it's your own friendships that are on the line. Moreover, I knew my friendships would inevitably change once everything was in the open, and wasn't sure I wanted that—I was happy with them the way they were.

The first person I told was my sister, the most liberal and left wing member of my family. She was very supportive, and let me know that she would stand by me when it came to telling my parents, lamenting how difficult it must have been for me growing up at home. Over the following few months I told my friends, in order of closeness, and my brother. They were all very understanding. Finally, I told my parents, with my brother and sister beside me for support, one Boxing Day morning.

After I told them, my mum burst into tears. Sobbing and juddering, she kept saying that it wasn't my fault, and my sister consoled her telling her it wasn't an issue of blame. I think my mum suspected it might have been her own fault. My dad sat in silence, but was visibly upset. The atmosphere was exceedingly uncomfortable and I was glad when I able to leave with my brother and sister, albeit with a sea of mixed emotions swirling around inside me. However, when I calmed down, the overwhelming feeling was one of relief; a great weight had been lifted from my mind. I had now told everybody close to me, and everything was in the open. From now on this was my identity, and people who met me would meet the real me.

Over the next year, I started experiencing all the things most people had been doing since they were teenagers, and eventually started seeing somebody. My parents had stopped enquiring about my personal life, which was frankly a relief after all the years of questioning about any female acquaintance. I was happy with my life. However, when I told my parents about my boyfriend on Boxing Day the following year, I was again met with grief. It was like I had come out all over again.

I was annoyed that my parents had always been so happy for any of my brother's and sister's relationships, but evidently not for mine. It turned out that, even though I made it clear when I came out that I'd known I was gay for years and it wasn't just a phase, my parents had continued to hope otherwise and had been praying that I be healed throughout that year. All those hopes had just been crushed by my revelation. Nevertheless, they asked to meet my boyfriend, and that was a start.

I introduced them to my boyfriend a few months later, and it went quite smoothly, all things considering. My mum seemed relaxed and more like herself, but my dad seemed a bit uncomfortable. Not renowned for his tact, as he left he blurted to my boyfriend, "*it's been such a relief to meet you—when our son first told us he was seeing a man, we had all kinds of visions!*" I let my embarrassment at this comment slide—the important thing was we were making progress.

The turning point happened the following Christmas. My dad and I were in the car alone, and after some hand-wringing, he said, "*when you first told us about being gay, your mother and I didn't really understand it.*" (He wasn't kidding: my mum had worried that I might catch it from my gay friend in the sixth form.) He continued to tell me about a gay minister who also suffered from "this gay problem," but he had married a woman and done extensive work on trying to "cure" gay people. I started to feel prickly—was he about to broach the subject of conversion therapy for me?

However, it turned out the minister had later admitted that he had been unable to cure himself or anybody else, and his marriage was effectively a sham in the sense that it was not a marriage in the normal sense of the word but a mutually agreed arrangement for companionship. This had prompted my dad to study scientific research into homosexuality, and realise people were probably born that way. The problem was with the Church; Christians themselves needed to be educated into changing their opinions. He concluded triumphantly by announcing that that he and my mother were now "gay-affirming". Although the awkwardness of the conversation made me cringe, it marked a welcome shift in my dad's attitudes towards homosexuality.

From then on, every time I visited home I would find replies to letters that my dad had been writing to church ministers scattered around, or article cut-outs about homosexuality. While my mum had become more moderate in her faith, my dad was becoming obsessive in his determination to make the church understand. Things reached a head when I declined to read a book about homosexuality and the Christian faith. My dad erupted in anger at my unwillingness to understand his religion, and we ended up having an argument about it.

It wasn't that I didn't believe in the Bible because I felt rejected by its teachings on homosexuality; I just didn't find it credible in a scientifically enlightened age, and I have my own moral compass. Therefore, what the Bible says about homosexuality didn't feel relevant to me. Nevertheless, whenever I had any problems, my parent's advice was always the same: have faith in the Lord, and the Lord would provide; whenever anything good happened, it was because they had prayed to the Lord, and the Lord had provided. I was tired of them pushing their religious views on me.

Given how central religion had been in my dad's life, it came as a surprise the following year when he told me that he now identified as an atheist. His letter writing campaign to ministers had fallen on deaf ears, and he'd found what it was like to be on the other side of the entrenched views and bigotry of the Church. Moreover, he'd done an in-depth study of the Bible and found that he could no longer reconcile its teaching with his own personal beliefs. He had reached his own conclusions, and finally seemed much calmer and accepting.

After he retired, my dad told me he had started writing a book about his experiences. A part of me felt frustrated that my sexuality should still warrant so much comment after all these years. However, when you move in a social circle where being gay is accepted, it's easy to forget that not everybody has that luxury. Furthermore, with all the focus on the gay person's experiences, it's easy to forget that sometimes the parents of gay children need support too, especially if, like mine, they belong to a religious community which is unable or unwilling to help.

In the years since coming out, I've been much happier. I'm more confident, my friendships are fuller, and my relationship with my parents has healed. My parents seem more at peace, after the strain of the past few years. The notion that people choose their sexual orientation is ridiculous, and given that love and relationships are such an important part of life, to try to

deny these things to a group of people because of your own moral convictions is simply wrong and should not be acceptable. I hope that any parent reading this, who may be struggling to accept their own child's sexuality, will find the help they need.

Homosexuality: The Bible on Trial

(The Sequel to Our Gay Son)

David Robert-John's sequel to *Our Gay Son* takes a close look at the New Testament to examine just how much orthodox belief can be derived from its teachings with any degree of confidence. How much unequivocal support does it give to the crucial ideas of the Virgin Birth, the miracles of Jesus, the Ascension or even the Resurrection of Jesus? How much credibility can be given to Luke's account of The Acts of the Apostles?

The author's views are thought provoking and controversial in places, and do not provide any comfort for traditional believers. However, it is his opinion that every believer should be confronted with these issues that are so often swept under the carpet in the interests of maintaining the faith. The fact that Christian beliefs have been held for two thousand years is no guarantee of their truth.

The Author would be more than delighted to discover any credible answers to the issues that he raises.